hooting Bears.

LEWIS & CLARK

LEWIS & CLARK
And the Crossing of North America
David Holloway

EXCALIBUR

Designed by Margaret Fraser *for*
George Weidenfeld and Nicolson Limited
11 St John's Hill, London sw1 1
and Saturday Review Press
201 Park Avenue South
New York, N.Y. 10003

ISBN: 0-525-700226
Library of Congress Catalog Card No: 73–75733

Printed in Japan

Contents

Introduction

THIS IS AN EPIC STORY of exploration which is rightly honoured in the history of the United States. Every continent has had its explorers, and there have been many whose names are associated with North America. Yet it is surprising to realise that as late as the first decade of the last century there was still a need for a major expedition to establish whether there was a usable route across the continent by water. The idea was President Thomas Jefferson's and it was he who, in 1801, appointed Meriwether Lewis to command it. Lewis in turn chose William Clark to accompany him, and together they became joint leaders. The success of this dual leadership was remarkable, and perhaps could only have been achieved because of their previous long-standing friendship.

In 1803 the party assembled at St Louis, where the Mississippi and Missouri Rivers join. There the boats were prepared and the men practised rifle shooting. These simple preparations are indicative of the times; they were to rely entirely on their own skills, both in travelling and to provide the greater part of their food. Self-sufficiency and determination were imperative, and to this end the leaders set about embuing the party with a sense of discipline and mutual confidence. On 14 May 1804 the 'Western Expedition' set out.

Jefferson's most detailed instructions required not only the seeking of a waterway but reports on the country, its inhabitants, its vegetation and the animal life. From time to time the expedition encountered both French and English traders from across the Canadian border, but for the most part they travelled through unknown territory, encountering only Indian tribes never before seen by white men.

By 4 November they had reached the country of the Mandan

Indians and settled down for the winter, near to the point where Bismark, North Dakota is today. Here they recruited two French Canadians, one with a Shoshone Indian wife – Sacajawea, the Bird Woman. Since she was sixteen years old and pregnant, it is surprising that the leaders allowed her to join; but their decision proved very wise, for repeatedly her presence gave confidence to the Indians they were to meet. Indeed, her personal contribution to the expedition may well have meant the difference between success and failure The birth of a child they all took in their stride, and she and her son completed the entire journey.

The story is one of tremendous tenaciousness and great physical endurance in the face of difficulties none had foreseen – not the least of which were problems with unreliable Indians. Having reached the head-waters of the Missouri they were forced to take to horses to cross the Rockies. Although by then it was clear that no waterway to the Pacific Ocean could exist, they pressed on and finally reached the coast on 15 November 1805, by canoe down the Columbia River.

Disappointed at finding no ships or white people at the end of their journey, they were forced to retrace their steps overland arriving back at St Louis on 23 September 1806. Despite an initial rather lukewarm approach, in the end their success was acclaimed by Congress. Although Lewis and Clark had proved that no waterway to the Pacific existed, they had opened up the huge hinterland to the west. For the United States the importance of the expedition was incalculable, both politically and commercially. In the world at large it ranks high in the field of human endeavour and discovery.

V. E. Fuchs

Author's Note

Anyone writing about American Indians encounters the
problem of what to call them. Most of the tribes have several
different names and it is not possible to be consistent. I have
quite arbitrarily chosen the names that seem to me the best
known, so I have used a mixture of Indian (Aricara), French
(Gros Ventres) and English (Blackfeet) to describe the various
nations. As for names of individual people, I have left them in
the original when they are easily readable (Sacajawea and
Cameawhait, for instance) but translated them when they are
a long jumble of syllables.

All those members of the Lewis and Clark expedition who
left behind written records had highly individual notions of
spelling. It seemed a pity to alter these unless a word was
totally unreadable. Clark in particular had a gift for a vivid
phrase which it would be a crime to change.

Partial View

1 'You Will Proceed...'

St. Louis

IT ALL BEGAN, like so many American dreams, in the mind of Thomas Jefferson. As private citizen, diplomat, politician, Secretary of State and finally President, he was always intensely curious. If something was unknown, he wanted to find out about it. And there beyond the Mississippi, the western frontier of the newborn United States, lay the vast unknown mass of Louisiana; not the modern state of Louisiana, but the central strip of North America. From it could come not only the marauding bands of Indians who harried the frontier settlements but also an invading European army which might drive the citizens of the new nation into the Atlantic. Jefferson wanted to know what there was in this region. Even more, he wanted to find out if there was a usable water route across the North American continent, another version of that abiding dream, the North-West Passage.

In 1792 Captain Robert Gray, an American, had brought his ship *Columbia* to the mouth of a great river running into the Pacific. He named it after his ship and laid claim to it as United States territory. If no further action was taken, it was doubtful whether this claim to the territory round the Columbia river could be supported. Captain Cook and Vancouver had both visited the area earlier, though it is unlikely that either of them had put into the river mouth. But the possession of land on the west coast formed an essential part of Jefferson's long-term plans. In the 1760s and 1770s visionary Americans like Robert Rogers were discussing the possibility of a water route across the continent. Basically the idea was this: there must be a continental divide, probably corresponding with what had been heard from the Indians about a range called the Rock or Rocky Mountains. If they could take a boat up to the head-waters of the Mississippi – an idea quickly abandoned when they found that it went due north rather than north-west – or the Missouri, which looked much more promising, there was no reason why within, say, twenty miles ('a single day's portage' was Jefferson's theory), they should not launch their boats on the Columbia river and shoot down to the sea.

Should this route prove feasible Jefferson, a life-long hater of the British, would have won a considerable victory. All the riches of the Orient could be brought direct across the Pacific, and carried by river across America to the United States. The monopoly of the British East India Company would be broken and the economy of the United States would be made much

more stable. But in the 1790s, when Jefferson was brooding about these problems, there were complications, mostly political. The principal of these was that Louisiana did not belong to the United States. Until 1762 this mostly unexplored land – roughly the whole area between the Mississippi valley and the Rocky Mountains below the 49th parallel – was French, except for Texas and New Mexico, which were Spanish. After that date, by the treaty which ended the Seven Years War, it was handed over to Spain. The English colonists of the East had got on well enough with the French, who allowed them to float their crops down the Mississippi and tranship them to bigger vessels at New Orleans for export without paying any customs duty. This policy was continued by the Spanish, but by the Treaty of Ildefonso (1800) Napoleon forced the beaten Spaniards to cede Louisiana back to him.

Napoleon discussing the Louisiana purchase treaty with Talleyrand and Marbois; an engraving from a painting by A. Castaigne.

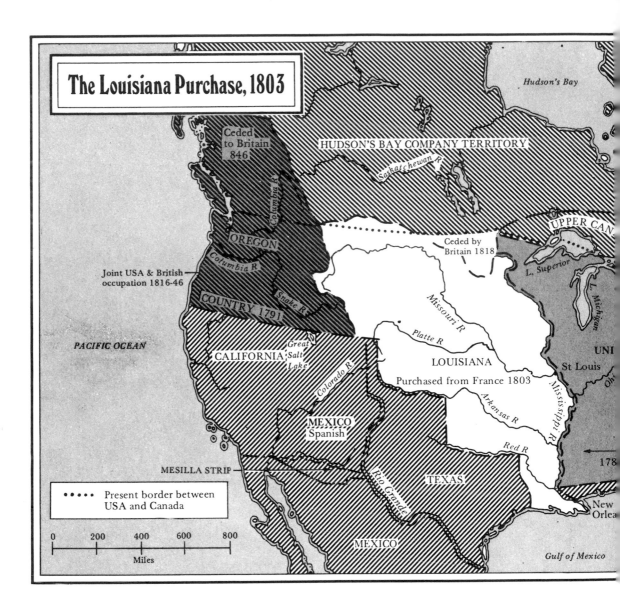

The Louisiana Purchase, 1803

Ceded to Britain 846

Hudson's Bay

HUDSON'S BAY COMPANY TERRITORY

Saskatchewan R.

Ceded by Britain 1818

UPPER CAN

Columbia R.

OREGON

Joint USA & British occupation 1816-46

L. Superior

Columbia R.

Snake R.

COUNTRY 1791

Missouri R.

Platte R.

L. Michigan

PACIFIC OCEAN

CALIFORNIA

Great Salt Lake

LOUISIANA

Purchased from France 1803

UNI

St Louis

Colorado R.

Ohi

MEXICO
Spanish

Arkansas R.

Mississippi R.

MESILLA STRIP

Rio Grande

Red R

TEXAS

178

····· Present border between USA and Canada

New Orlea

| 0 | 200 | 400 | 600 | 800 |

Miles

MEXICO

Gulf of Mexico

PREVIOUS PAGES Before the white settlers came, the Indians relied on the great buffalo herds for their main food supply. This famous painting by Charles Russell shows a typical hunt. A dead buffalo belonged to whoever's arrow was found in the carcass.

This transfer was to be the corner-stone for the creation of a great French empire in the New World. Napoleon's all-conquering army was to land in the south and, proceeding up the Mississippi, conquer the United States and recover Canada. A large force was embarked. On the way it was to put down a slave revolt on the island of Santo Domingo and punish its leader, Toussaint L'Ouverture. It got no farther than this yellow-fever ridden island. The slave revolt was

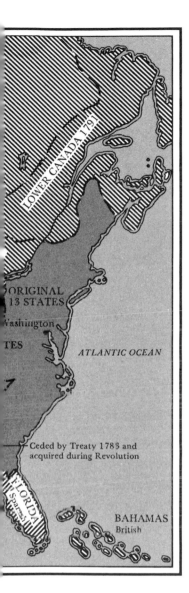

temporarily checked but 17,000 men died in the process, mostly from sickness. Napoleon lost interest in the New World, so much so that he wanted nothing more than to get rid of his stake in it. Jefferson, who was by now President, promptly sent his Secretary of State, Madison, over to France to negotiate the sale of Louisiana. What really concerned him was New Orleans: whoever controlled the mouth of the Mississippi ruled the whole river. Somewhat to the Americans' surprise, however, the French wanted to sell the whole area. No one knew how big it was, for the frontiers were totally undefined over large sections, but it proved to be something over 880,000 square miles. And for it the United States paid just fifteen million dollars – something like four cents an acre.

So by July 1803 Jefferson knew that the political difficulties were solved. He could at last freely send an expedition to seek his water route across America. But, being Jefferson, he had not wasted his time earlier on. Ten years before this he had made his first move, just one year after Gray discovered the Columbia river. He decided to send a secret expedition of just one observer and a servant to prospect the route.

The first man to volunteer to go on this trip was a nineteen-year-old friend of the Jefferson family, Meriwether Lewis. A Virginian by birth, he had been trained by a schoolmaster – a close friend of Jefferson's – to think in terms of territorial expansion, and his ambition was to be an explorer. Quite properly Jefferson turned this young army officer down; he was not experienced enough. The man he chose was André Michaux, who had been on Captain Cook's voyage up the Pacific coast. He was to go alone, or with one other man, to avoid alarming the Indians; and, in order not to provoke the Spaniards by starting too near their territories of Texas and New Mexico, he was to set off from the west coast, making his way in the first place south-eastwards from the Columbia river. This meant he had to cross the Atlantic and travel right across Europe and Asia before he could get to his jumping-off point. The capricious Catherine the Great of Russia, after granting Michaux a passport to cross her territory, later withdrew it so that he was stuck there and unable to make the voyage. So Jefferson's first plan lapsed.

While this was going on, other events were happening in the north. The North West Trading Company – the London-based concern that controlled the fur trade in the western part of

Sir Alexander Mackenzie (*c.* 1755–1820), the Scottish-born Canadian explorer, who led the first overland party across the Rockies to reach the Pacific in 1793; portrait by Sir Thomas Lawrence.

Canada – was also becoming interested in exploring the American continent, though it is doubtful if they would have done much about it but for the enterprise of one man, Alexander Mackenzie. In 1789 Mackenzie had made his first attempt to reach the Pacific, using the Canadian rivers as his highway, but he had taken the wrong turning and found himself in the Arctic. In 1793 he managed to reach the Pacific coast. It was a heroic journey; the rivers that he used were just passable in small canoes, but the extreme difficulty of the passage through the mountains made it totally impossible to use this route for general trade. His account, published in the late 1790s, showed that the Scottish traders and the Frenchmen who worked with them were interested in the north-west and were striking down from Canada to the northern waters of the Missouri.

Mackenzie's success made it all the more important for Jefferson to mount an expedition. In 1801 he became President of the United States. One of his first actions was to appoint Meriwether Lewis, now a captain in the First Regiment of Infantry, as his private secretary. On the face of it, this was an extraordinary choice. Lewis, though of good family – his mother was a connection of George Washington – was no civil servant. Since his late teens he had been in either the militia or the regular army. He had seen service in the Whisky War against Indians who refused to pay taxes. He was renowned as a hunter and a naturalist, but was not the man who would be expected to make a good private secretary to the President, unless, that is, the President wanted a man close to him in whom he could confide his plans for exploring the west. Obviously he had kept his eye on Meriwether Lewis and signed him on as soon as he could.

We do not know quite how soon Jefferson and Lewis started making their plans. Certainly by 1802, while the negotiations were going on for the Louisiana purchase, Jefferson was asking the Spanish minister to the United States if the Spanish Court 'would take it badly, that the Congress decree the formation of a group of travelers, who would form a small caravan and go and explore the course of the Missouri River'. The Spanish minister informed his Foreign Secretary in Madrid: 'I replied to him that . . . an expedition of this nature could not fail to give umbrage to our Government.' He was not deceived about Jefferson's motives, for he added: 'The President has been all his life a man of letters, very speculative and a lover of glory,

Meriwether Lewis from a
portrait at Independence
Hall, Philadelphia.

and . . . he might attempt to perpetuate the fame of his admin-
istration . . . by discovering the way by which the Americans
may some day extend their population and their influence up
to the coasts of the South Seas.'

In fact this rebuff did not matter much, for the Louisiana
purchase was almost complete. Even before the treaty was
signed, Jefferson sent a secret message to Congress asking for
the appropriation of $2,500 to pay for an expedition consisting
of 'an intelligent officer with ten or twelve chosen men'. The
party would try to make its way 'even to the Western Ocean,
have conference with the natives on the subject of commercial
intercourse, get admission among them for our traders . . . and
return with information acquired in the course of two summers'.
With the backing of Congress, Jefferson then formally appointed
Lewis to take command of the expedition. As much of the

OPPOSITE The raising of the American flag at New Orleans to mark the official transfer of the Louisiana territory from France to the United States on 20 December 1803.

expedition's purpose was to be scientific, he despatched his secretary to take a crash course at Philadelphia in botany, zoology and the study of Indian culture.

In April the President handed to Lewis the rough draft of his instructions. These ran to several thousand words, showing the interest that Jefferson took not only in the idea of the project but in the practical details of it. It seems probable that, if he could, he would have loved to go along himself. Indeed, in Lewis he had picked a man as like himself as he could find to be his representative. So the President set down not only general directions: 'The object of your mission is to explore the Missouri river, & such principal stream of it, as, by its course & communication with the waters of the Pacific Ocean, offer the most direct & practicable water communication across the continent, for the purposes of commerce' but also minor points:

Your observations are to be taken with great pains & accuracy, to be entered distinctly, & intelligibly for others as well as yourself, to comprehend all the elements necessary, with the aid of the usual tables, to fix the latitude and longitude of the places which they were taken . . . several copies of these, as well as your other notes, should be made at leisure times & put into the care of the most trustworthy of your attendants, to guard by multiplying them, against the accidental losses to which they will be exposed, a further guard would be that one of these copies be written on the paper of the birch, as less liable to injury from damp than common paper.

And so on, right down to such tiny details as that:

Other objects worthy of notice will be . . . climate as characterized by the thermometer, by the proportion of rainy, cloudy & clear days, by lightning, hail, snow, ice, by the access & recess of frost, by the winds prevailing at different seasons, the dates at which particular plants put forth or lose their flowers, or leaf, times of appearance of particular birds, reptiles or insects.

The President was perfectly aware of the hazards of the enterprise and saw that the double journey across the continent and back might prove too difficult, for he made it clear that if the party reached the Columbia river and could not face the return journey they should wait until a boat arrived to pick them up. Otherwise, they could send back two men by sea with an account of the expedition's adventures while the rest headed home as best they could by the way they had come.

And a grim note authorised Lewis to nominate his successor, should he fail to complete the journey. In the event of another taking command, he too was immediately to nominate *his* successor 'to provide, on the accident of your death, against anarchy, dispersion & the consequent danger to your party, and the total failure of the enterprise'.

Now Lewis could think about recruiting his party. He appears not to have hesitated at all, for on 19 June he was writing from Washington:

Dear Clark:

From the long and uninterrupted friendship and confidence which has subsisted between us I feel no hesitation in making to you the following communication under the fullest impression that it will be held by you inviolably secret . . .

'Dear Clark' was William Clark, who, like Jefferson and Lewis, was a Virginian, the ninth child of parents who had moved over the Cumberland Gap into Kentucky when he was a boy. There he had grown up on the frontier. At eighteen he was an ensign in the US Army and three years later he was appointed a lieutenant in the infantry. He saw service in the Whisky War with Lewis; it is possible, though not certain, that they served for a short time in the same unit. In 1795 Clark fell ill, and a year later he resigned his commission to become a farmer. He was at work in Clarksville, Kentucky, when Lewis's letter arrived. We cannot be certain how well Lewis and Clark knew each other, but Clark wrote years later to the editor of the journals of the expedition to say that he had visited Lewis often in Washington before the trip and had met Jefferson.

The post to Kentucky was slow. It was over a month before Clark received Lewis's invitation, and presumably nearly as long before his reply reached Washington. Lewis, keen to get started, was already making proposals to other possible companions before Clark's letter arrived, but withdrew them when he saw what Clark had written:

I will cheerfully join you in an 'official character' . . . and partake of the Dangers Difficulties & fatigues, and I anticipate the honors & rewards . . . should we be successful in accomplishing it. This is an immense undertaking fraited with numerous Dificulties, but my friend I can assure you that no man lives with whom I would prefer to undertake and share the Dificulties of such a trip than yourself.

William Clark.

Clark agreed to bring with him men he thought suitable for the trip. Tough men, used to living the rough life of the frontier, would serve them best. It was agreed that about half the party should be serving soldiers and that the others should be volunteers from the frontier areas who would be paid the same wages as private soldiers (five dollars a month) plus various allowances for clothes.

Within a month Meriwether Lewis was on his way via Pittsburgh to St Louis, the village that stood at the junction of the Mississippi and Missouri rivers. When the party gathered there, it suffered two slight disappointments. First, Congress, perhaps to spite Jefferson for the high-handed way in which he

expected them to rubber-stamp the decisions he made, refused to honour the President's promise to gazette Clark as a captain in the infantry, which would have made him the equal of Lewis. They would only authorise his appointment as second lieutenant in the Corps of Artillerists. Lewis, however, always referred to Clark as 'Captain'.

The other disappointment was perhaps a blessing in disguise. When, at the end of 1803, Lewis presented himself to the Spanish resident commander at St Louis, and informed him that the expedition was going to set off up the Missouri, the Spaniard denied any knowledge of the Louisiana purchase and refused permission. This setback had the unexpected result that while the muddle was being cleared up, the expedition's members had a chance to settle down and get to know each other. It was probably a good thing that the teething troubles noted by Clark in his diary – clashes of personality and so on – were settled before the trip started. The men practised endlessly with their rifles – this was vital, for they were relying almost entirely on shooting for the pot to feed themselves – and they learnt discipline. Clark reported that he had 'tried' a number of the men for various offences. There were boats to build and provisions to prepare. Clark stayed at the expedition's camp at the mouth of the Wood river while Lewis hurried around on errands. Three boats were prepared: a keelboat fifty-five feet long, drawing three feet of water, carrying one large square sail on a mast amidships, and with provision for twenty-two oars; and two pirogues, flat-bottomed boats shaped like flat-irons which could hold eight or ten men and would generally be rowed or poled along, one by six oars, the other by seven.

TOP LEFT A drawing from Clark's field note-book of the keelboat that was used for the first part of the voyage, showing its shallow draught and pointed ends. It could be sailed, rowed or poled along. The painting by Felix Achille St Aulaire (above) is of a larger, more refined version but of similar design.

However, it would be possible to hoist an oar and use the pirogue's canvas cover as a sail when the wind was aft, to give the oarsmen a rest.

Great care was taken with the packing. The success of the expedition depended on husbanding its resources. It was essential that the twenty-one bales and two boxes should have balanced contents, so that if one was lost the expedition would not be left without its whole stock of a given commodity. Each bale was packed to contain a little of everything, though one box was reserved for presents for the Indians who would be met with on the way. All these preparations took longer than might have been expected, and it was not until four o'clock in the afternoon on 14 May 1804, that the party of forty-five set sail. It was raining at the time.

Captain Lewis & Clark

...ding a Council with the Indians.

As the party makes its first four miles up the wide Missouri, it is perhaps time to introduce them. The expedition was probably unique in having two commanders of equal status who never argued and who allowed each other exact equality. Often scouting ahead was needed. Without any question one of them would go ahead while the other brought on the main force. Roughly speaking they took turns, but there does not seem to have been any fixed rule about this. On vital decisions they always agreed, although they were obviously very different people. Meriwether Lewis was better educated, more volatile, more of a worrier. Jefferson described him in a memoir as being a hypochondriac, but there is little sign of this in the log of the expedition; he seems to have suffered no more ill-health than any other member of the expedition. He was the better speech-maker, and when they had parleys with the Indians it was usually Lewis who did the talking.

Clark was the perfect complement to this. He was red-headed, with the fiery nature that often goes with that characteristic. At one vital moment, when a rowdy band of Sioux tried to hold on to one of the boats after it had been cast off, he lost his temper and drew his sword on them. Nevertheless, he was a rock of good sense at the centre of the expedition's councils. He seems to have been liked equally by the white men and the Indians. When at various times the two leaders were attending to the ailments of the Indians they met, Lewis noted that it was Clark who was 'their favourite doctor'. Certainly, as he was to prove in later life, he had a great sympathy for and understanding of Indians. Even twenty years after the expedition came back, it was always to the 'red-headed One' that the Indians appealed for justice, and when he could, he saw that they got it.

It has not been possible to discover what Lewis and Clark called each other. In their letters it was always either 'Dear Lewis' or 'Dear Friend'; in the journals they always referred to each other punctiliously as 'Captain', though often with the addition of 'my good friend'. Whether they used each other's Christian names we shall never know.

Though not the next in the chain of command, the most useful member of the expedition, in that he was the best woodsman and hunter, was George Drewyer. This spelling is the one used by the leaders in their journals. His real name was almost certainly Georges Drouillard; he was the son of a

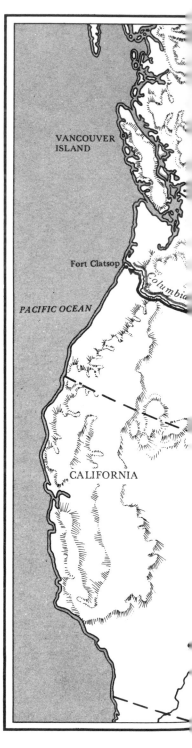

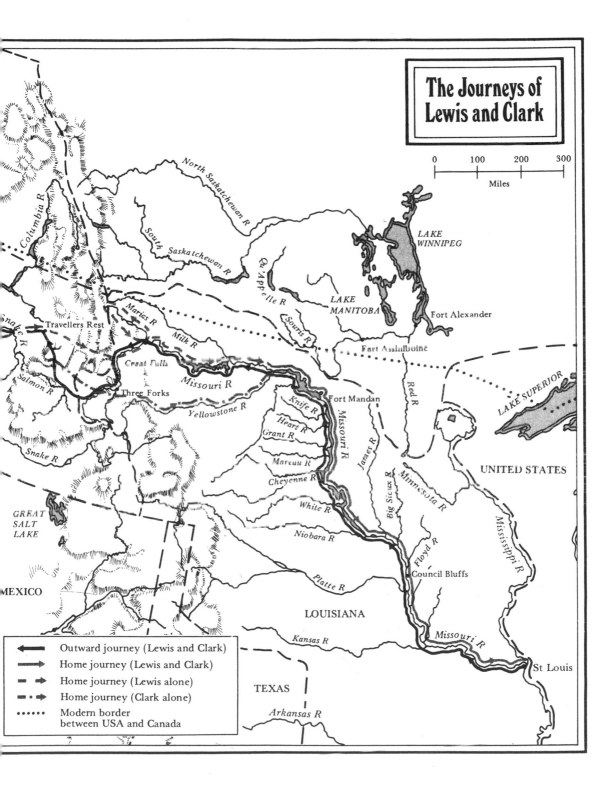

The Journeys of
Lewis and Clark

0   100   200   300
Miles

North Saskatchewan R

Columbia R

South Saskatchewan R

Qu'Appelle R

LAKE WINNIPEG

Souris R

LAKE MANITOBA

Fort Alexander

Travellers Rest

Marias R

Milk R

Snake R

Salmon R

Great Falls

Three Forks

Missouri R

Yellowstone R

Knife R

Heart R

Grant R

Mareau R

Cheyenne R

Snake R

White R

Niobara R

GREAT SALT LAKE

Platte R

Fort Mandan

Missouri R

Red R

Fort Assiniboine

James R

Big Sioux R

Minnesota R

LAKE SUPERIOR

UNITED STATES

Mississippi R

Floyd R

Council Bluffs

MEXICO

LOUISIANA

Kansas R

TEXAS

Arkansas R

Missouri R

St Louis

→ Outward journey (Lewis and Clark)
→ Home journey (Lewis and Clark)
→ Home journey (Lewis alone)
→ Home journey (Clark alone)
...... Modern border
       between USA and Canada

French Canadian father and an Indian mother. He was almost always a member of the scouting parties ahead, his magnificent shooting helping to fill the cooking pot. As an interpreter he was the highest paid of the subordinates, receiving $25 a month.

Three sergeants (paid $10 a month) were each in charge of a mess. They were John Ordway – who seems to have had special responsibility for the horses – Nathaniel Pryor and Charles Floyd; the last-named was destined to be the expedition's only casualty. It is not necessary to list the rest of the names at this stage. Some of the men never emerge from the background of the story and one deserted early on; in fact, only twenty-eight of the original party took part in the full journey, with some additional recruits picked up on the way. The ones most often mentioned are the Fields brothers, Joseph and Reuben, who were good hunters; William Bratton and John Shields, both skilled as blacksmiths and gunsmiths; and Francis Labiche and Peter Cruzatte, both of them primarily boatmen. And there was John Coulter, who played no particularly special part in the expedition but was later to achieve fame as the discoverer of the source of the Yellowstone river. He won a secure place in American folklore when, captured by Blackfeet Indians near Beaver's Head on the Jefferson river, he was given the chance of saving his life by outrunning some five hundred pursuers. Stripped naked, he was given enough start for him to out-distance most of his followers; only one got near him, and Coulter was able to grab this man's spear and kill him before diving into a river and hiding for the rest of the day under driftwood, up to his neck in water. Then he was faced with a seven-day walk to the nearest settlement. He made it. This shows the sort of physical toughness characteristic of the members of the expedition.

Most of them were in their twenties. All the soldiers and the Kentucky men were unmarried. One, George Shannon, was only seventeen when the expedition set out. He was, as the Victorian historian of the expedition said rather primly, the one member of the party that Meriwether Lewis might have expected to meet on the same social terms. He was certainly trusted to do a full man's work and was often sent off by him-self on errands. Unfortunately he had a very poor sense of direction and was always getting himself lost. Somehow, though, he managed eventually to rejoin the main party, hungry and cheerful. Incidentally, he was the one member of

A Canoe striking on a Tree

the expedition to have a successful later career. He became a lawyer and subsequently a judge and a state senator in Kentucky. He might have gone further and entered federal politics had he not died at the age of forty-nine.

We only need mention two more of the party. These were Peter Gass, the carpenter, rather a bad lot but a good man to have around in a tight spot. He had been a soldier and was older than most of the others. He was elected sergeant after Floyd's death. And there was York, Captain Clark's Negro slave who, for no pay at all, made the full journey. His black skin and woolly hair caused great astonishment and at times a little awe among the Indian men, and his sexual prowess was admired and sought after by their womenfolk.

So the boats set off, where possible sailing but more often rowing against a current that could at times be very strong. When, as could happen every day or so, there were rapids, most of the occupants of the boats would have to get out and tow, hauling on long lines that were always liable to break. It was not all easy going; the first rapids showed them how little they knew about cargo stowage. Too much weight in

One of the lively and often inaccurate woodcuts illustrating Peter Gass's *Journal of Voyages* (1812), the first account of the expedition to appear in print.

31

the stern made the big boat almost unsteerable. They ran aground on sandbars and had to leap into the water to push the boats off. The mast of the big boat was broken when they swept under an overhanging tree. Oars were snapped on rocks. Although for the first fifteen hundred miles the travellers were going up what was in effect the high road to the north-west, they had a rough ride. Still, there were compensations. The Osage Indians, who lived on the banks of the river some two hundred miles above St Louis, were friendly. The expedition reckoned to feed itself, and two horses were being led up the bank for use by the hunters when Lewis and Clark agreed to buy a deer from the Indians for two quarts of whisky; a deal they must have regretted later, since the expedition ran out of spirits more than a year before its return.

By mid-June they were well settled down. Most days they managed to make something like twenty miles upriver, but sometimes the wind was too high and they had to lie up. They spent such times drying meat for later use or making oars, from ash-wood when they could find it, to take the place of those broken in coping with rapids.

On 26 June they had an unpleasant experience. The Missouri had narrowed right down as it passed through a canyon and was running very fast. The tow-rope snapped as the big boat was being pulled through and the boat was badly damaged on sharp rocks. It might well have been lost if two men had not swum out with another rope. This necessitated a two-day pause for repairs. And then a week later the mast broke again.

The battle with the river was not the only excitement. The party's discipline was put to a stern test. Sergeant Floyd, the guard commander, charged one of the sentinels, John Collins, with being drunk on duty and allowing Hugh Hall to draw whisky from the common stock and get drunk also. Collins was found guilty and sentenced to a hundred lashes while Hall, who pleaded guilty, was let off with fifty. If the commanders had not imposed strict discipline at this point they would never have been able to rely on the absolute obedience of this party of roughnecks in more dangerous circumstances later on. It is indeed noticeable that once the party was slimmed down and the real work of exploration began, such 'trials' were a thing of the past.

Their journey had now taken them past the junction of the Kansas and the Missouri rivers, where Kansas City now stands, and they were heading up towards the Platte. On their left were the great Kansas prairies, and it was in this country (near what is now Aitchison) that they celebrated the first Fourth of July of their journey. (A year later they were to drink the last of their whisky to celebrate the day near the source of the Missouri and the year after that, split into two parties and surrounded by unfriendly Indians, they had no time to celebrate at all.) In this first flush of their enthusiasm they fired off morning and evening guns. Each man was issued with an extra gill of whisky and they danced to the fiddle played by one of the French boatmen as they were camped in what Sergeant Floyd described in his highly individual spelling as 'one of the Butifules Prairies I ever Saw open and butifulley Divided with Hills and vallies all presenting themselves'.

The only blot on a happy day was that Joseph Fields was bitten by a snake; but 'Doctors' Lewis and Clark cured him with a poultice of bark and nitre which presumably drew out the poison, since he seems to have recovered quickly. He was not the only casualty. Another man was very ill with sunstroke. The universal remedy of a dose of nitre plus a 'bleeding' by Lewis cured him, but a couple of days later the trip had to be halted because five men were suffering severe headaches.

On 14 July the expedition very nearly came to a sudden end. The three boats were rowing calmly up river when a squall of high wind accompanied by thunder and lightning suddenly placed the craft in grave danger. The big boat would have been dashed to pieces against rocks if the better part of its crew had not jumped into the water and fended her off. The waves were washing over the weather side and would in the end have swamped the boat, but after forty minutes the storm stopped as suddenly as it had begun and the river became as calm as glass. The two pirogues were half a mile ahead in a safer stretch of water, and though tossed about escaped damage. That evening the party saw their first elk, the largest of the deer family, which was to supply so much of their food later on.

A week later they had arrived at the mouth of the Platte river. There was plenty of evidence that Indians lived in this area – burial mounds, abandoned lodges and so on – but now they saw their first positive proof, an Indian dog trotting along the bank. The time was come for Lewis and Clark to put into operation one of the main tasks of the expedition, which was to show the flag and open trade negotiations with the Indians.

33

Herds of buffalo and elk which were found in great numbers on the plains.

ABOVE and OPPOSITE
Clothing and belongings of
Prairie Indians living beside
the Missouri, sketched by the
Swiss artist Karl Bodmer.
The large skin robe shows a
typical Sioux illustration of a
battle. Other objects include
ceremonial pipes, drum,
tambourine and adornments
made of buffalo skin, weasel
fur and eagle feathers.

There were two tribes based around this area. The Ottoes
were the remnant of a once large tribe who now lived under
the protection of the other tribe, the Pawnees. Drewyer and
Cruzatte were sent off with presents of tobacco to visit the
permanent villages of these two peoples. It was an abortive
trip, for the men were away hunting buffalo, so the party
went on its way. A few days later two of the hunters brought
back a Missouri Indian they had found by the way. He agreed
to act as an ambassador while the expedition made camp by
a large rock which they called Council Bluffs. This was not
where the present town of Council Bluffs, across the river from
Omaha, stands, but some twenty miles to the north of it.

Here Lewis and Clark's first delegation of Indians eventually
arrived. The party was headed by six chiefs, three each from

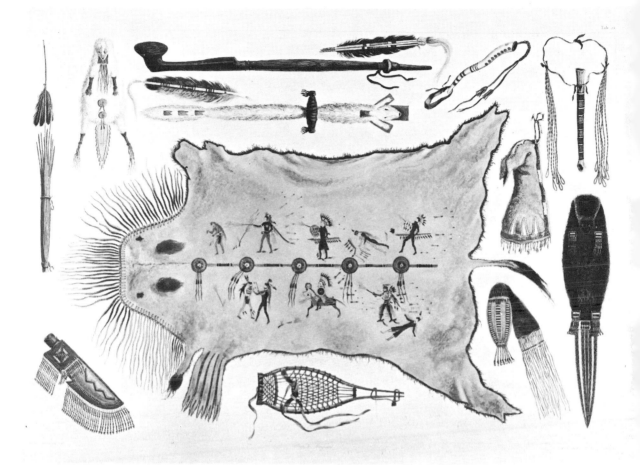

the Ottoe and Missouri nations, and with them came a French
interpreter who lived with them as a trader. A canopy was set
up under a tree and the swivel gun on the big boat was fired in
salute. After preliminary courtesies a council was agreed on for
the next day. Then Lewis and Clark had their first taste of
Indian speech-making. After Lewis had opened the proceed-
ings by announcing the change of government, that the Great
White Father (the President) would give them his protection
and that they must now trade with the Americans, each of the
six chiefs made a lengthy speech in reply. It all boiled down to
an agreement to trade, a request for guns to fight their enemies
the Omahas, and a complaint that they had never got anything,
not so much as a single knife, out of the French without paying
for it.

The expedition was quick to take up this hint. The visitors were presented with an American flag, a laced coat to take back to the paramount chief, who had not come, and medals of different grades for the chiefs who had. The explorers also handed out, with a liberality they were later to regret, gunpowder and whisky, as well as trade goods like paint and dress ornaments. Clark wrote in his diary: 'They was well content with what they Recd in the presence of their two fathers, which was M. Lewis and Wm Clark.' That evening the expedition rowed off, happy that its first effort at empire-building had been a success.

Even so, things still did not go smoothly. First Sergeant Floyd was sick, and then there was the awkward incident of Moses Reed, one of the soldiers in the party. He had had enough of the expedition. Pretending that he had lost his knife, he wandered off. When he did not turn up that evening a search party was sent back to look for him. They came back with him a couple of days later, saying that he had deserted and was making his way home. He was probably hoping to hitch a lift from one of the traders heading downriver in the autumn with their supply of beaver pelts. A court-martial was immediately convened and Reed was found guilty. He was ordered to run the gauntlet of the entire expedition four times while each man flogged him as he passed, either with a bundle of nine switches or with their rifle ramrods. On top of this there was the further penalty that he was no longer to be considered a member of the expedition. He would have to stay with them until the big boat was sent down, but he was to be 'in Coventry'. This sentence was carried out, even though three visiting chiefs begged that he might be pardoned.

Such was the impression made on the Indians by the first council that more of them arrived to pay their respects. Lewis and Clark were now entertaining the head chiefs. Little Thief, the paramount chief of the Ottoes, handed in the medal he had been given by the French and received in its stead the largest medal that the expedition could supply. While Little Thief was happy enough with his gifts, there was a certain amount of grumbling among the others. One received only a certificate, promptly handed it back to 'Big Blue Eyes' (Clark) and was given a sharp lecture. The certificate was handed over to the head chief to give 'to the one he thought most worthy'; with great tact he returned it to the man who had rejected it.

The council broke up with a dram of whisky all round, and the expedition prepared to start again. Sergeant Floyd now became violently ill. It seems probable that his attack of illness at the beginning of the month was the preliminary grumbling of appendicitis. Now the organ had perforated. The 'doctors' could only guess that it was (in Clark's spelling) 'biliose chorlick'. Medicines did no good, and Floyd died bravely on 20 August. He was buried with full military honours on a bluff near what is now Sioux City, Iowa, and a cedar post carved with his name was raised to mark the spot. The expedition had suffered its first fatal casualty barely two months after it had set out. Not even the most optimistic member of it would have dared to predict that no one else would die before they returned home. Yet this was what happened.

The next day they were on their way again. This time it was Lewis's turn to risk his life. Jefferson had asked him to send back a report on the minerals they found on the way, so he landed on a bluff and started to make a geological survey. He found alum, copper, cobalt and pyrites, but in testing for cobalt he nearly poisoned himself with arsenical fumes. But, tough man that he was, he took a dose of salts and felt better. This stern remedy left him rather weak. When, the next day, he set off with Clark to explore the country around, he could not keep up and they had to make camp.

They wanted to explore, for they were now in the vicinity of a number of Indian holy places. One was the grave of the great chief Blackbird, who had terrorised the area for years and had, like so many others in the region, died in the smallpox epidemic of four years before. Blackbird had been buried sitting upright on horseback under a great mound of earth. The expedition hung an American flag on a nearby tree in his honour. This chief was supposed to have magical powers of killing people, but one cynical writer has said that he owed his fame to having secured a supply of arsenic from a passing trader.

They also visited a more attractive place on the Great Sioux river, which runs into the Missouri, where a great red cliff stands from whose clay all the Indians of the neighbourhood made their pipes. This was a sacred place; there could be no fighting near it and a fugitive could find asylum there. The official record of the trip comments pompously: 'Thus we find even among savages certain principles deemed sacred, by which the rigours of their merciless system of warfare are mitigated.'

The artist George Catlin set out from St Louis in 1830 and followed the same route as Lewis and Clark up the Mississippi and Missouri. His journal, which included these drawings, was published in 1841 and is an invaluable record of the life and customs of the Indian tribes.

ABOVE The stone quarry whose red clay was used by the Indians to make pipes.

LEFT The Missouri·river with its cliffs and overhanging trees that were such a danger to the canoes.

ABOVE The grave of the
Omaha chief, Blackbird.

BELOW The grave of
Sergeant Floyd, the only
casualty of the expedition.

G. Catlin   Myers & Cº 20

The third place that they visited was also sacred, but since it was supposed to be inhabited by evil demons eighteen inches high none of the neighbouring Indians – Sioux, Omahas or Ottoes – would go near it except to sacrifice. It stood in a flat plain, forming a great parallelogram of earth, a hundred yards long and twenty yards wide, rising to a flat top seventy feet high. Indian tradition claimed that the little people were experts with bows and arrows and killed anyone who went near. Keeping a sharp lookout Lewis and Clark climbed to the top, but were happy to report that they saw no one, though there was evidence that human sacrifices had been made there within the last few years.

The various incidents that have been mentioned took place in the first few months of the trip, but it must not be thought that something happened every day. Basically the life of the expedition was a hard, monotonous grind. At first light they were up and pushing off the boats, and most of the day was spent sweating at the oars. Thirty-five men were needed for rowing; if one takes into account the two hunters ashore, the helmsmen and the two commanders, this means that there was little rest for anyone. Most days there would be a time when they would have to form a line to haul the boats along by the tow-ropes. In the evening they would find a suitable place for camp, divide into their messes for cooking, and take their turn at guard duty. During this part of the trip, they ate well. On 21 August they killed their first buffalo and the hunters also brought in quantities of elk and deer. What they could not eat, they 'jerked' – drying it and making it into a concentrated lump rather like South African biltong.

As they proceeded northwards, the prairies became even more abundant in game. They saw and killed their first antelope, which they referred to as a 'goat', and also shot a variety of birds. Some they captured alive, including a pelican. In a spirit of scientific enquiry they filled its beak with water and found that it could hold five gallons. Another animal which they saw for the first time was the prairie dog, the gay little burrowing animal which stands on its hind legs (which is why the expedition thought it was some species of ground squirrel). Prairie dogs proved remarkably elusive, but eventually one was caught and its skin and skeleton preserved to be sent back to Washington.

What spare time the members of the expedition had was

spent in swatting the mosquitoes which came in clouds every night, doing running repairs on clothes and, most important of all, dressing the skins of the animals. The clothes they started with were rapidly wearing out and the travellers would soon have to rely entirely on buckskins and moccasins to clothe them. For entertainment there was the fiddle, and on every festive occasion there was dancing. The commanders and the sergeants had the additional duty of keeping their journals. Every day the position had to be checked and meteorological observations made, and on the one occasion when they let the chronometer run down there was the laborious business of calculating the time exactly by astronomical observation.

As August turned into September, they realised that it was going to take longer than they thought to reach the Mandan villages that were their objective as a winter stopping-place. The whole party would have to winter upriver, as there would not be time for the military escort and the French boatmen to get back to St Louis before the river froze over. As they were now entering Sioux country they could not afford to do without the extra fire-power of Corporal Warfington and his six men, who were not intended to be part of the main expedition, and the French watermen were needed to take back the big boat laden with the specimens gathered on the first leg of the expedition.

Lewis had been specifically instructed by the President to deal with the Sioux. The traders who travelled up and down the waterway had been complaining for some time that one of the divisions of the Sioux nation, the Tetons, had been virtually closing the river and demanding heavy payments before they would allow any boats through. The Sioux were relative newcomers to this region; they had been driven west by the Chipewas and were now trying to dominate the Omahas and the Ottoes of the neighbourhood. In addition Jefferson had another reason for wanting the Sioux to be impressed by American might; they had always been in the past allies of the British trading companies in the north, and the President was determined that they should look east to Washington for their patronage rather than north to Canada. So Lewis gave orders for the prairie to be set on fire, the customary signal for inviting Indians to a council.

As the party reached the mouth of the James river, an Indian swam out to one of the boats and told them that a large party of

Prairie dog. Lewis, never having seen such an animal, described it as a barking squirrel.

Yankton Sioux were camped nearby. On 27 August, Sergeant Pryor and two men were sent with an invitation to the Indians to hold a council. The Yankton, a more peaceable race than their Teton cousins, received the sergeant with great honour. They proposed to carry him into their village on a buffalo robe – the highest honour they could offer – but he refused it because he was not an officer. He accepted, however, the gift of a whole roast dog. Whatever doubts he may have had when he started on it, he set them aside and reported that the meat was well flavoured. A grand council was arranged for two days hence, and Pryor set off, accompanied by five chiefs and seventy warriors.

This was the first big Indian village that the expedition had come across. It consisted of conical lodges made of poles covered with buffalo skins painted white and red. Each of them could accommodate ten or fifteen people and had a fire in the centre, the smoke from which escaped through a hole in the roof of the tent. This fire was purely for heat; the cooking was done in a lean-to at the side. Lewis and Clark liked the look of these men; they had 'a certain air of dignity and boldness'. They were dressed in buffalo robes and leggings over breech cloths and were fond of decorations. Some of them wore necklaces of bears' claws three inches long and all of them were painted and wore porcupine quills and feathers in their hair. Most were armed with bows and arrows, but a few had ancient fowling-pieces. The visitors noticed that some of the younger men sat apart. These were the men whose role the US Cavalry were to know well in the Indian wars of sixty years later – the Dog Soldiers, a special society who swore never to retreat. Lewis and Clark recorded admiringly that when twenty-two of these men had recently gone into battle with the Crow Indians, eighteen had been killed and the other four had had to be dragged from the battle by their friends. But the explorers also noted that this refusal to go otherwise than straight forward had its foolish side. They were told of a party of these braves crossing the ice: one fell through, and the others went on and were drowned as well rather than go back or round about.

Lewis and Clark chose an open space under a big tree for the council and unfurled the flag as Shake Hand, the paramount chief of the Yanktons, came up with his subordinate chiefs, White Crane, Struck by Pawnee and Half Man. (It is assumed, by the way, that the name of the last mentioned did not imply

44

any lack of virility on his part but showed modesty in naming himself; in other words, he was not claiming to be a great warrior.)

The first meeting went well. After the ceremonial smoking of a pipe of peace, Lewis made his usual speech about the United States taking over protection of the Indians and handed out his presents – a big medal, the laced coat of a lieutenant in the Corps of Artillerists and a cocked hat with a red feather for the head chief and smaller medals for the lesser ones. The chiefs held a private meeting and said they would reply the next day, so the rest of the time was spent in jollity. The Indians showed their skill in archery. Lewis was not much impressed, noting that he had seen other Indians shoot much more accurately, but he gave a prize to the winner. Then the dancing began, long hours of a shuffling dance to the accompaniment of a drum and rattles made of buffalo-hide casings with stones inside them.

The next day, after another ceremony of pipe-smoking, Shake Hand rose to speak. A Frenchman who lived with the Sioux acted as interpreter. The English and the Spanish had given him medals, the chief said, 'but nothing to keep it from my skin; but now you give me a medal and clothes. But still we are poor; and I wish, brothers, you would give us something for our squaws'. After the other chiefs had spoken, one of the warriors got up to say that what they really wanted was 'Great Father's milk' (whisky), but the burden of all the speeches was that they were poor and needed traders to bring them goods and guns. If this happened they were ready to make peace with the nearby nations and to send representatives to Washington to show their good will. Lewis and Clark handed out more presents in return for an agreement that Sioux representatives would go to Washington the next year.

It was not much, but it was as much as they could expect. At least they parted from the Yanktons with good will on all sides. The next day they set off again and for a week or so made their way upriver. The buffalo were now very thick on the ground and they estimated one herd at five hundred beasts. The young George Shannon gave his first demonstration of how easily he could get himself lost. During the night the two horses used by the hunters wandered off and he was detailed to fetch them. He found them, but assumed that the party had got farther up the river than in fact they had and

45

Painting by Karl Bodmer of a Sioux camp at Fort Pierre, showing the tightly wrapped body of a dead chief exposed on a platform. After the spirit had been given a chance to escape, the body was buried in the ground.

47

pressed on ahead of them. It was not for over a week that he realised he was going the wrong way and turned back. On the sixteenth day after losing the party he found them again. He had had to abandon one of the horses as it was exhausted and he was nearly starving. He had run out of bullets the fourth day, but had managed to kill a rabbit by firing a bit of hard stick instead of a ball. For the rest of the time he lived on grapes. He was so desperate that just before he sighted the party coming up the river towards him he had decided to kill the second horse.

For a couple of weeks the party continued up the river without incident. They rounded the great bend of the Missouri where the river goes almost round in a circle, past Cedar Island where a French trader had his post. On 24 September they got their first indication that they were in Teton Sioux territory. Coulter was ashore acting as hunter. As he was stalking game, his horse, the only surviving one, was stolen. The main party came on a group of five Sioux by the river. Lewis ordered action stations and anchored away from the land. The interpreter shouted ashore that the expedition came in a friendly spirit but they were not afraid of the Tetons and they wanted their horse back. It was intended as a present for their chief, but they would not talk to him until the horse was returned. The five Sioux denied any knowledge of the horse but said that if they found the horse they would return it. Lewis and Clark were not entirely reassured by this and sent one of the Indians to tell their chief that they wanted to parley. The other Indians were allowed to sleep by the shore under a guard consisting of one third of the party, who also kept an eye on the two small boats, which were drawn up on the shore. The rest slept with their weapons by their sides on the big boat.

The next morning the whole party came ashore and paraded in military fashion, all carrying guns. The flag was raised as Black Buffalo, the head chief, arrived, with Partisan, his second-in-command, two other chiefs and about fifty warriors, and, incidentally, without the horse. They were a remarkable sight. Their heads were shaven, only a centre strip being left, and the hair from this braided behind. In their hair they wore feathers and porcupine quills. From the head of the main chief hung a long string of golden eagle feathers. They agreed to smoke the pipe of peace, but when Lewis tried to make his speech he found that none of his party could speak Sioux

Catlin painting of a buffalo hunt. The conical hills in the background were one of the unusual features of the terrain that Lewis and Clark commented on.

Sioux Indian showing the customary centre strip of hair braided behind: painting by A.J. Miller. The handsome bearing of the Sioux much impressed Lewis and Clark.

sufficiently well to get his message across. He had to cut the speech short, but handed over the customary presents and ferried the chiefs and some of the warriors out to the big boat to show them the swivel guns and other fittings.

He gave Black Buffalo a quarter of a glass of whisky which the chief liked, demanding more in a rather drunken way. When Lewis showed him the empty bottle, he sucked it lovingly to try and get the last drops. Then Partisan, who had also been given a drink, pretended to be very drunk and protested when the party tried to send him ashore. He said he had not been given enough presents, and refused to leave. What is more, he said that the expedition would go no farther. The threat was a serious one; Lewis and Clark had been told by the French trader they had passed on the river that Partisan was the bully who exacted the tariffs from traders. Clark got the chiefs into one of the pirogues and headed for shore, Partisan still declaring they would go no farther. Clark's red-headed temper began to rise. As he recorded in his diary: 'his justures were of Such a personal nature I felt my self compeled to Draw my Sword.' He also signalled to Lewis on the big boat. Lewis trained the swivel gun to point towards the shore and ordered his party to aim their rifles at the chiefs. For their part, the Indians strung their bows and tried to seize the rope of the pirogue. It was a test of nerve. The two parties stood staring at each other. Had either Lewis or Clark weakened for a moment it would have been all over. Even if they had not been killed on the spot, they would have had to pay tribute and would certainly have depleted the resources of the expedition to such an extent that it might never have reached the Mandans, let alone the Pacific. But since they received no signal from their chiefs, the Indians did not notch arrows into their strung bows, and the chiefs climbed ashore. As he walked away, Partisan shouted that he had plenty of warriors and would kill them all by degrees. Clark shouted back with the aid of one of his men who could speak a little of the Sioux language that he could summon aid from the White Father of such deadliness that the whole of the Teton nation would be wiped out in an instant.

After this tense moment, there came a laughable anti-climax. As Clark and his men were rowing back to the big boat, a messenger from Black Buffalo swam out. 'Please,' he asked, 'could the squaws and children be allowed to see the wonders of the big boat, the next day?' The situation still remained tense, though, and most of the party stayed awake that night in case of a sudden attack, which did not come.

Next day Lewis went ashore with an escort. They had won the first round and it was time to consolidate their position. It was quite evident now that the Sioux were frightened, so when Black Buffalo suggested a council Lewis agreed. Clark came ashore and the two of them were carried ceremoniously on a huge decorated buffalo skin to a lodge big enough to hold seventy men. They all sat down in a circle. In the centre of the floor the Spanish flag was laid out beside the Stars and Stripes that Lewis and Clark had presented the day before. Beside these, on short forked sticks with swan's-down scattered on the ground around them, rested the red clay pipe of peace. After an elder of the tribe had made a long speech begging for pity,

Black Buffalo lit the pipe with great ceremony, pointing the bowl north, south, east and west before smoking it and passing it to Lewis, who in his turn smoked it and passed it on. Then the Sioux presented the expedition with four hundred pounds of buffalo meat. A fire was lit to prepare a grand feast of roast dog and pemmican mixed with potato. The visitors tasted the dog meat out of courtesy but enjoyed the pemmican. They ate off platters with horn spoons. There followed a long display of dancing; first the warriors jumped up and down and then the squaws shuffled to the sound of a tambourine. Each squaw

A Sioux camp with the painted conical lodges covered with buffalo skins that were the homes of this tribe.

carried the scalps of the men her husband had killed. At midnight the party broke up, and as a sign of mutual trust four minor chiefs went down to sleep on board the big boat.

Next day the squaws came to visit the boat. They wore their hair long and parted in the middle, either loose or tied back. Their loose, sleeveless skin dresses were fastened with string at the shoulder and sometimes with girdles at the waist. If two of the women had a fight they were separated by the village policeman, who wore crow feathers as a badge of his office. This post, which carried supreme power, even over the chiefs,

53

Lewis and Clark were fortunately never threatened by the possibility of scalping although they saw plenty of evidence of the custom in the way squaws wore round their waist the scalps taken by their braves in battle.

The upper half of this diagram shows the ways in which scalps were displayed by the Indians. Below, the scalping operation itself.

was held by each man for only a few days before it was passed on to another.

The tension between the two parties was rising again, particularly after Cruzatte, one of the French boatmen, discovered some Omaha prisoners and spoke to them in their language. They told him that they were convinced that the Tetons would not let the American party continue, and were planning something. There was more dancing that evening, but when the party set off back to the big boat an inexperienced helmsman fouled the main anchor rope in the darkness and the rope parted. There was confusion and a great deal of shouting. Some of those on board thought the Indians had cut the rope and the Indians thought that they were being attacked by their enemies. Both sides spent an unquiet night, but by good fortune they did not start attacking each other.

The anchor being lost, the big boat had drifted from its relatively safe position in the centre of the river to near the shore. Though Lewis and Clark were keen to get under way as soon as possible, they spent some time looking for the anchor, but could not find it. They gathered stones to act as a substitute and packed up ready to leave. At first the Indians on board refused to leave, but eventually all but Black Buffalo were bundled off. Then several of the Indians hung on to the ropes attaching the boats to the land, refusing to let go. It was another showdown. Lewis and Clark did not hesitate; they told their men to make ready to fire at the men holding on to the ropes. Black Buffalo hastily intervened, saying that the men only wanted tobacco. They were given some and the boats set off, the chiefs still demanding flags and more tobacco. They were refused the flags but some tobacco was thrown to them.

As a guarantee of safe conduct, one chief remained on board. When, the next day, the boat hit a log and nearly overturned he got frightened and demanded to be set ashore. He assured the explorers that they would not be molested again, so they set him ashore with the present of a knife and a blanket.

It was now October. The weather was getting very cold, and the party worked its way up the river as fast as it could. They would not stop when some Indians called out to them from the shore but pressed on, past the house of a French trader and some abandoned Indian villages, looking for the next major Indian nation that they must meet, the Aricaras. On 8 October, they found these people camped on a large island in the river, living a pastoral life with fields of tobacco, corn and beans. Lewis and Clark were not sure of their reception, so while Lewis went with the interpreters to the village, Clark made camp on the shore with doubled sentinels, as well as leaving an armed guard on the big boat. A council was arranged for the next day, but the weather was so bad that it could not take place. The boats were battered by the waves; the only things that could ride comfortably on the water were the bull-boats, round coracle-like boats made from a single buffalo-skin stretched over a wooden frame, in which the Aricara squaws bounced around on top of the high waves. The expedition would see many more of these later in the month, when they arrived at the Mandan villages.

This Aricara village was used as a centre by French traders

A later artist's impression of York, Clark's slave, on display in a Mandan hut. The Indians had never seen a black man before. They 'examined him from top to toe' and some of the women tried to rub off what they assumed was black paint.

and a number of them were present. This made the translation problem easy. For the first time the party discovered that it had a secret weapon in dealing with the Indians, one that they were often to use later. The Indians were fascinated by York, Clark's Negro slave. They could not believe that he was not painted black, though they were convinced of his naturalness when he took off his hat and showed them his woolly hair. York, who was a considerable character and in every way – except that he was not paid – a full member of the expedition, put on an act for the Aricaras. He told them that he was descended from wild animals and had been tamed by his master. In addition he demonstrated, with much grunting and grimacing, how strong he was.

Chiefs were called in from the nearby villages for the council, which went on cordially for two days. The expedition presented the Indians with a steel mill for grinding their corn and in return received presents of vegetables. One thing that marked the Aricaras out from the other Indians they met was that they refused whisky. They were surprised, they said, that their Father should present them with a liquor that would turn them into fools. These, Lewis and Clark felt, were good Indians. They were polite and obliging. When asked if they would send representatives to Washington, they said they would be delighted to but they were frightened of the Sioux. This was a pattern that the party was to come across time after time: the Sioux bullied the Aricaras, the Gros Ventres did the same to the Mandans and so on.

Another thing that disposed the expedition in favour of the Aricaras was the obligingness of the squaws. This is best described in the rather prim prose of the official history of the expedition, based on the diaries of Lewis and Clark:

These women are handsomer than the Sioux; both of them are, however, disposed to be amorous, and our men found no difficulty in procuring companions for the night by means of interpreters. These interviews were chiefly clandestine, and were of course to be kept a secret from the husbands and relations. The point of honor indeed is completely reversed among the Ricaras [Aricaras]; that the wife or the sister should submit to a stranger's embraces without the consent of her husband or brother is a cause of great disgrace and offence, especially as for many purposes of civility or gratitude the husband or brother will themselves present to a stranger those females and be gratified by attentions to them. The Sioux had offered us squaws, but we having declined while we remained there, they followed us with offers of females for two days. The Ricaras had been equally accommodating; we had equally withstood their temptation; but such was their desire to oblige us that two very handsome young squaws were sent on board this evening, and persecuted us with civilities. The black man York participated largely in these favors; for, instead of inspiring any prejudice, his color seemed to procure him additional advantages from the Indians, who desired to preserve among them some memorial of this wonderful stranger. Among other instances of attention, a Ricara invited him into his house and, presenting his wife to him, retired to the outside of the door; while one of York's comrades who was looking for him came to the door, but the gallant husband would permit no interruption until a reasonable time had elapsed.

However obliging the Aricaras and their squaws were, the cold winds and the occasional snow in the air reminded the expedition that it must be on its way again. Perhaps it was the stay with the women of the village that had upset things, perhaps the change in the weather, but on 13 October John Newman, one of the private soldiers, was arrested for a 'mutinous expression' and was tried the next day. He was sentenced to receive seventy-five lashes and to be discharged from the party and sent home. An Aricara chief who had come with them as a peace-envoy to the Mandans was most upset at the idea of corporal punishment and burst into tears. Clark recorded: 'I explained the cause of the punishment and the necessity [of it] which he thought examples were also necessary, & he himself had made them by Death, his nation never whiped even their Children, from their burth.'

The sentence was carried out. Poor Newman tried very hard to get the sentence of discharge from the party reversed and worked assiduously during the winter at Fort Mandan. Indeed on one of the hunting trips he became so badly frostbitten that he might have been permanently disabled. Lewis and Clark refused to reverse their decision but relented to the extent that they sent back a message with him that he was to be paid up to the moment of his discharge and that should the expedition be successful he should be given half of what would have been his share in the rewards at the end. (One of the inducements to go on the trip was that the members should be given grants of land when they returned.)

On they went through the prairie land, which swarmed with game, great herds of buffalo and elk; in one group of elk two hundred and forty-eight head were counted. Deer and antelope were plentiful as well, and the hunters thought nothing of killing fourteen beasts in one day. The weather was getting still colder and several of the men were complaining of rheumatic pains. The worst hit was Clark, who was almost totally incapacitated for several days by rheumatism in his neck. Lewis did his best to relieve the pain by placing a hot stone on the affected part but it did little good. They were coming close to the Mandan villages now, and the river was becoming almost crowded with French hunters and agents making towards this centre of trade. Some of the voyagers complained that their beaver traps and some of their pelts had been stolen by Sioux. Certainly there were marauders about. From the river Lewis and Clark saw one party of a dozen Sioux dressed only in breech clouts, obviously a war party. The Frenchmen travelling with them thought that the Indians were after Mandan horses. Clearly the expedition had not far to go to reach their appointed winter stopping-place. On 25 October they saw a big hunting party which turned out to be made up of Mandan Indians, including one of their grand chiefs. As Clark was still unfit, Lewis went ashore alone with the Aricara chief who had come with them. They were all immediately on good terms, and the Aricara decided to go by land with the Mandan party to their main villages about four miles away.

The next day most of the expedition went ashore to hold their first council with the great chief, Big White, and to make the customary exchange of presents. The chief in return came to inspect the boat. The two things that impressed the Indians most were York and a grinding mill that was fitted into the structure of the boat.

Now all the expedition had to do was to find a suitable place to build winter quarters. Clark found a bit of bottom land about a mile downriver from Big White's village, which was one of five in the neighbourhood, two of which belonged to the Mandans, one to the Ahnahaways and two to the more belligerent Gros Ventres. For the first time for five months they started building themselves quarters on land. The long first leg was over. Since May they had travelled sixteen hundred miles, and had now reached the point where the river turned due west and followed a course that no white man had ever seen. They would have to wait for spring before they could set out again.

Bodmer's painting of a Mandan village with
women poling bull-boats – made from basket
work covered with buffalo hides. They were
used as runabouts for crossing the river or
for short journeys.

3 Winter

IT WAS ESSENTIAL FOR THE EXPEDITION that it should establish good relations with the local people if its members were to rest easily through the winter and lay in the necessary supplies for the next leg of their trip. In fact they started off on the wrong foot by accident. William Clark, still suffering from his painful neck, could scarcely walk. He smoked a ceremonial pipe, but refused to go to a banquet. This was taken by the Mandans as an insult, and a lot of tact was needed to persuade the Indians that no slight was intended. Eventually, under an awning rigged to shield the participants from the gale, a grand council was called. This was an important meeting because the expedition was in disputed territory close to the 49th parallel, and Hugh MacKendrick, an Irishman working for the North West Company, was in residence in the village. One of the tasks that Lewis and Clark had been set was to ensure that trade went down the Missouri to St Louis rather than east and north to the North West's trading posts. Before they set out, Jefferson had given them a letter from the British Minister in Washington as a *laisser-passer*. This they now handed over to MacKendrick to transmit to his superiors. At the time he made no protest, but left a couple of days later for his winter quarters in a fort farther north. A more subtle attempt at asserting British rights was made in the spring when the party prepared to move; the North West Company demanded the right to send a British observer along. This was firmly turned down by Lewis and Clark.

At the Grand Council, Lewis had to establish American suzerainty. He did this in a long speech, not only recommending the Missouri trade but demanding that anything taken from the traders in the past year by the Mandans and the Gros Ventres should be returned. He confirmed various chiefs, including Big White and Coal, as heads of their villages and nominated Black Cat as the grand chief of the whole Mandan nation. Black Moccasin was to be head of the Gros Ventres, and Wolf Man Chief was to be head of that tribe while Black Moccasin was away at war with the Snake Indians. There was the usual exchange of presents and a demonstration of the firing of the swivel gun.

The Mandan villages were quite unlike any other Indian homes that the expedition had seen. Here the tribes lived as a settled community, or at least tried to. Originally they had made their homes some sixty miles down the river in large

PREVIOUS PAGES Every winter the Missouri froze sufficiently hard for it to become the main highway. A Mandan village is in the background.

communities, but like most of the other Indian tribes they had
been ravaged by smallpox and their numbers considerably
reduced. Then they had been driven north by the arrival of the
Sioux, but now they had settled down again. They did not live
in tents but in large conical buildings with the floor below
ground level. The main structure was made of timber over
which was piled earth, so that the whole looked like some huge
round-topped sandcastle set on the flat ground. As the weather

was so cold in winter, each of these huts had to be large enough to contain not only several families but also the horses that had been trained for the summer buffalo-hunts and the supplies of dried meat and corn that the families might require during the winter. Round the whole village a wall of earth and timber was built as a protection against outside attack. The expedition could be fairly certain they would not be in danger from these people, but like them they would have to protect themselves against the Sioux by building a fort.

On 2 November the first cottonwood tree was chopped

Catlin's painting of a Mandan village showing its conical huts made of wood and earth. Unlike many other Indian tribes in the North West, this people lived in a settled community, with solidly constructed buildings surrounded by protective ditches and palisades.

66

down. The fort was to consist of two rows of huts built at an angle to each other, each hut to contain four rooms, fourteen feet square and seven feet high, with a plank ceiling and a sort of loft above. The outside walls were to be eighteen feet high, and to complete the triangle on the side where there were no buildings there was to be a picket fence of the same height. The main buildings took about three weeks to put up, but it was Christmas Day before the commanders hoisted the flag to show the completion of the work.

As Lewis and Clark settled into their quarters visitors began to arrive, and the expedition was to gain some valuable men with local experience. One of these was Baptiste Lapage, a French Canadian who had lived with the Cheyenne in the Black Hills; he was signed on. Other traders with their squaws also moved in for protection, and finally another French Canadian came to offer his services. His qualifications consisted principally of having a sixteen-year-old Shoshone or Snake Indian for a wife. Between them they would make a valuable addition to the team. So they were signed on, and the expedition gained its folk-heroine. Sacajawea came from the royal family of the Snake Indians. She had been captured by a raiding party six hundred miles up the Missouri and had been brought back as a slave. Toussaint Charbonneau, a man in his thirties with several wives, who had traded round these parts for years, had taken a liking to her and made her his wife in addition to the others. He wanted further adventures and this exploration seemed a good chance. The only trouble was that Sacajawea was pregnant. The baby was due in February and this meant that when the expedition started again in March, she would be travelling with a papoose on her back.

It may seem incredible that Lewis and Clark should have agreed to take her, but clearly the advantage of having a Shoshone-speaking member of the party outweighed everything else. Certain fictional accounts of the expedition have given her credit for making all the major decisions on which way to go, but this is obviously an exaggeration. It is certain, though, that she was constantly consulted for her local knowledge. Sacajawea – her name meant Bird Woman – was always described as 'gentle and modest', and seems to have been much appreciated by the other members of the expedition. When, as happened on various occasions, she became sick, they recorded her progress with care in their diaries, and the only

Sacajawea, the Shoshone girl who became the folk heroine of the expedition.

time they got angry with her was when, after one such bout of sickness, she went out and ate unripe fruit and made herself ill again. They might refer to her just as 'our Indian woman' or 'our Squaw' in their diaries, but they were clearly very fond of her. She was part of the expedition from mid-November.

At this time the first ice was appearing on the river, and several times it snowed all day. The hunters were bringing in as much meat as they could. After one long trip they arrived with thirty-two deer, eleven elk and five buffalo. All these were smoked to preserve them through the winter. The Mandans came in and out of the fort, trading and giving presents. Little Raven, one of the chiefs, arrived one day with a present of sixty pounds of buffalo meat, carried on the back of his squaw. Often, though, they brought rumours of a possible Sioux attack. Then one of the Gros Ventres came with an even more disturbing rumour. They had been told that the white men were planning to combine with the Sioux to attack the five villages. Why otherwise would the Frenchmen have left the Indian huts and gone to live in the fort? Lewis and Clark did their best to reassure their visitors, and noted in their diaries that no doubt the English traders and their spies were responsible for this *canard*.

The expedition was not allowed to settle down to the long snowy winter (thirteen inches of snow fell on 29 November alone) without further excitement. In the middle of one night there was a sudden shout from one of the sentries. He claimed that one of the Indians was trying to murder his wife close to the fort. When the guard turned out, and enquiries were made, it emerged that the woman had run away from her husband after a row and had been obliging members of the expedition with her favours while staying with Sacajawea and the other interpreters' wives. The Indian had come seeking his revenge. Lewis and Clark ordered Sergeant Ordway, one of those who had slept with the woman, to give the man some presents. After the Grand Chief, who happened to be sleeping at the fort that night, had spoken to them the couple went off, though, as Lewis noted, 'by no means in a state of much apparent love'.

November ended with a more serious alarm. A terrified Mandan arrived at the fort to say that his hunting-party had been attacked by a band of Sioux. Two men had been killed and several others injured. In addition, nine horses had been stolen. This gave Lewis and Clark an opportunity to show that they were ready to protect the villagers. Within an hour, Clark and a force of twenty three men had formed a protective ring around the nearby huts. The Indians were at first alarmed that the expedition was going to attack them, but when Clark told them he was ready to join them in pursuing and punishing the Sioux raiders, the Indians said that it was too late in the year but that they would be ready to go in the spring. This display of force deeply impressed them, and from this time on Lewis and Clark had no further trouble in making it clear which side they were on.

The snow lay deep and the river was frozen. The Mandans had to use dog sleighs to carry meat, but they decided there was a chance of one more buffalo-hunt. Clark and fifteen of the party went with the Indians and killed ten buffalo. In the event they only secured five of them, for when they went the next day to bring in the rest they found that they had disappeared.

OVERLEAF The dog sledges of the Mandans used to carry meat and other goods across the frozen river; by Karl Bodmer.

Fig. XXIX

The Indians explained that, according to their custom, if a buffalo was found dead without a personally marked arrow sticking into it, it belonged to the finder. Bullets did not count. Clark went out again; this time, to make sure that they kept all they killed, he stayed so late skinning the dead beasts that he and his party had to spend the night sleeping on the prairie in the snow, covered only by a single blanket apiece and the hides of the buffalo that they had skinned. The thermometer that night registered forty-two degrees of frost; several of the men suffered from frostbite. At the fort it was so cold that the sentries had to be changed every half hour.

On Christmas Day the flag was raised inside the fort for the first time. The day is best described in Sergeant Ordway's diary:

we fired the Swivels at day break & each man fired one round. our officers Gave the party a drink of Taffee [rum]. we had the Best to eat that could be had, & continued firing dancing & frolicking dureing the whole day. the Savages did not Trouble us as we had requested them not to come as it was a Great medician day with us. We enjoyed a merry cristmas dureing the day & evening untill nine oClock – all in peace & quietness.

The new year was ushered in with more firing of the boat's cannon, and to celebrate the day the expedition paid a round of calls on the Indian villages. They took with them the fiddle, tambourine and hunting-horn and put on a display of dancing for the Indians. Lewis and Clark were worried that the people of the other nearby village would feel slighted because there was no show for them, so they hurried over there with York, who put on a solo display for the second village. Clark reported that it 'amused the Croud Verry much, and Somewhat astonished them, that So large a man should be active &c. &c.'

A few days later it was the Indians' turn to dance. Their performance went on for three nights, and was not so much an entertainment as a complicated ritual to ensure plenty of buffalo for the next season. The official historian felt it necessary to record Lewis's account of the affair in Latin, but Clark's diary tells us what happened:

The old men arrange themselves in a circle & after smokeing a pipe, which is handed them by a young man dressed up for the purpose. [From pictures drawn by later visitors to the Mandan villages, it appears that this young man was dressed up in a buffalo-skin] the young

72

men who have their wives back of the circle go each to one of the old men with a whining tone and request the old man to take his wife who presents herself necked [naked] except for a robe and sleep with her. the Girl then takes the Old Man who verry often can scarcely walk and leades him to a convenient place for the business, after which they return to the lodge; if the old man (or a white man) returns to the lodge without gratifying the man & his wife, he offers her again and again; it is often the Case that after the 2d time without Kissing, the husband throws a new robe over the old man &c. and begs him not to dispise him & his wife (We Sent a man to the Medisan Dance last night, they gave him 4 girls) all this to cause the buffalo to Come near So that they may Kill them.

The weather was getting even colder. One night the thermometer registered seventy-two degrees of frost. The next day an Indian boy was brought to them with his legs completely frozen; he had spent the night out of doors with only a buffalo robe for cover. Lewis later had to amputate the boy's toes. But another Indian who had also spent the night in the open without a fire had no ill effects. Clark recorded with wonder: 'Customs & habits of those people has anured them to bare more Cold than I thought it possible for man to endure.'

It would be a couple of months before the expedition could start again. Much of their time was spent talking to the Indians who came to visit them, particularly the Gros Ventres, in an effort to build up as complete a picture as possible of the territory they would have to cross during the summer. From what they heard they learned that the original plan of going right up the Missouri and then carrying their boats a short distance and launching them into the Columbia river would not work. The Indians told them of big mountains and a great waterfall. They would certainly need horses, and the Shoshone Indians controlled the stock of them in that area. They would not be able to proceed without the good will of this nation. Sacajawea now became important for the forward planning. She claimed to be a member of the ruling house and could act, with her husband's help, as the necessary interpreter. Would she be fit for travel? Her baby was due in early February. They would just have to wait and see.

Meanwhile food was beginning to run short. The party not only needed food to keep them going through the winter, they had also to prepare stocks to take with them. The Indians were prepared to trade, and the two blacksmiths of the expedition

Dances of the Mandan Indians

The dances of the plains tribes embodied the very spirit
of their lives and were of a highly symbolic nature.
Dancers were chosen for their distinction in war or the
hunt and wore the tokens of their reputation in their
costumes. The horns of a dancer's headdress might be
painted a colour to indicate his bravery and spears or
shields used in actual battle might be carried. Before the
dance, a feast was held and the costumes and
headdresses to be used were displayed on a central pole
inside the dance lodge.

BELOW Dance of Mandan women, who are wearing
hussar-like caps made out of buffalo cowskin.

OPPOSITE Buffalo Dance: the most important of the
rituals which was designed to conjure the wandering
herds nearer to the encampments. In it the hunters act
out the killing of the animals.

74

Chief of the Gros Ventres
Indians of the Prairies.

were kept very busy making axes out of iron with holes punched in them for decoration. The Indians regarded these as beautiful, but their makers considered them inefficient. In return the braves sent their squaws with big bundles of corn. The regular surgery that Lewis and Clark undertook also brought payment in corn and other vegetables.

As the early February days passed the weather began to get a bit warmer, and the party tried to cut their boats out of the ice so that they could be got ready for the next stage of the journey. It was a hopeless task, as they were frozen inside and out.

Experiments were made with heating stones and putting them into the boats, but all the rocks they could find burst with the heat before they could be raised to the required temperature. The ice was still hard enough for the hunting-parties to make their way down the river on it in search of game. On 4 February Clark left with eighteen men on a trip that was to last for more than a week. He went twenty miles or more down the river, killing forty deer, three buffalo and sixteen elk. This haul, weighing in all some three thousand pounds of usable meat, was virtually the salvation of the party. The hunters came

Gros Ventres' camp on the banks of the Upper Missouri with a keelboat in the foreground. The traders, seeing a large party of Indians swimming towards them, have their guns at the ready.

Buffalo hunt on snow shoes
by George Catlin.

happily back and sent off five men, with Drewyer in command, to bring back the meat on horse-drawn sledges. They had not brought the meat in themselves because they were almost exhausted.

In sending so small a party to fetch the meat, Lewis made one of his rare mistakes. He knew that with the better weather Sioux raiding parties were on the move, and that they would be looking for small parties to rob. This is exactly what happened. Drewyer's little cavalcade was ambushed by about a hundred Sioux who cut the traces of the sledges and stole two of the three horses. Clark thought the chief of the party left the third horse because the white men did not immediately give in but started firing, so that the Sioux withdrew to decide whether to kill the party or not. While they were doing so, the men beat a hasty

78

retreat with the remaining horse, abandoning most of their equipment.

When they got back to the camp, Lewis prepared to leave at first light with twenty-four men, at the same time sending word to the villages asking for support. Most of the village men were away hunting, but Big White and a few others turned up. The pursuers were too far behind the Sioux to catch them but they chased them to the point where they had camped for the night, and then gave up. The horses were gone, but the raiders had not found Clark's main stock of food. Lewis brought this back with him, together with some extra deer carcasses that he and the others had shot on the way.

While this excitement was going on, another equally exciting event was taking place in the fort. At five o'clock on the evening of 11 February, Sacajawea gave birth to a son. Lewis noted in his diary that night the arrival of 'a fine boy', adding:

It is worthy of remark that this was the first child which this woman had boarn, and as is common in such cases her labour was tedious and the pain violent; Mr Jessome [one of the French traders who was living temporarily with the party in the fort] informed me that he had frequently administered a small portion of the rattle of a rattle-snake, which he assured me had never failed to produce the desired effect, that of hastening the birth of the child; having the rattle of a snake by me I gave it to him and he administered two rings of it to the woman broken in small pieces with the fingers and added to a small quantity of water. Whether this medicine was truly the cause or not I shall not undertake to determine, but I was informed that she had not taken it more ten minutes before she brought forth.

By the end of the month they were able to get first the two pirogues and then the big boat out of the ice and draw them up on the shore. They had to use a windlass and an elk-skin rope that kept breaking. It was clear that the big boat would be of no use to them in the upper stretches of the river; they would have to build a number of canoes, each to hold about five men, for the haul up to the headwaters of the Missouri. Some five miles from the fort there was a plentiful supply of cottonwood trees, the best for use in canoe construction. This task would delay their departure, but it would free the big boat to take the specimens they had collected and their copious notes on the Indians and the flora, fauna and geography back to St Louis for transhipment to Washington.

As the weather improved a number of British traders began

2263
1609
654

Burnt Poles Creek

Camped 17th of May 1805

Camped 16th of May 1805

Course & Distance 19th May 1805

S 85° W. 1¼ to a point of woodland on the
  Lard. side opposite to a bluff S.S.

South 1½ to a point of timber on the Stard side
  opposite a bluff - high hills on L.S.

S 25 W. 1 mile to a point of woodland Lard. side
  opposite to a bluff

S 40 E. 1½ to a willow point Stard. the river
  making a deep bend to the E.

S 20 W. 1 along the Stard. side opposite to a bluff

N 80 W. 2½ to a point of woodland Lard. side opposite
  to a bluff

North 3/4 along the Lard. shore opposite a

S 30 W. ½ along the Lard. point opposite to a bluff

S 15 W. 3 to a point of woodland Stard. opposite
  to a bluff the river making a bend to East

S 22 W. 1½ to a point on Lard. side low

S 45 W. 3/4 to the point of high land

North 1 3/4 to a point of willows Stard opposite a bluff

to appear on the scene, again bringing news from the outside world. One such item, telling of the amalgamation of two rival British trading companies in Canada, made it all the more important that the American expedition should be a success and should firmly establish the United States as the authority in the Upper Missouri river. It is probable that if Lewis and Clark had failed, and still more if they had had to come back with their tails between their legs, the British companies would have got such a firm hold on the area that when the time came for frontier demarcation they would have been almost impossible to shift. It is possible to discover some sort of picture of what Lewis and Clark were like at this time from a letter written by one of the visiting Britons, Charles McKenzie:

Mr La Rocque and I became intimate with gentlemen of the American expedition, who on all occasions seemed happy to see us, and always treated us with civility and kindness. It is true, Captain Lewis could not make himself agreeable to us. He could speak fluently and learnedly on all subjects, but his inveterate disposition against the British stained . . . all his eloquence. Captain Clarke was equally well informed, but his conversation was always pleasant, for he seemed to dislike giving offence unnecessarily.

Despite all the civilities, the British traders were certainly doing their best either to join the expedition or to wreck it. For one thing they tried to persuade Charbonneau to cry off, which would have meant that Sacajawea would not have gone either. He came to Lewis with a set of impossible conditions – he would not be under the orders of the Americans and so on – so they dismissed him. However, after a couple of days, presumably as a result of some persuasion from the other Frenchmen going on the trip, he changed his mind and offered his services unconditionally.

By the last week in March the six new canoes were finished. They were carried the mile and a half to the river for launching. The ice was really thawing now that the temperature was staying above freezing point. This breaking up of the ice gave the Indians a chance for a peculiarly merciless bit of hunting. They drove buffalo towards the water, and as the huge beasts clattered on to the thinning ice they fell through, leaving them at the mercy of the Indian spears and arrows. The braver hunters dashed across the breaking ice to reach their quarry, then paddled to safety on an ice floe. This slaughter helped to stock the expedition's larder.

OPPOSITE Page from William Clark's notebook showing a map of a section of the Missouri river and the camps of the outward and homeward journeys.

81

BELOW Sioux bear dance, by George Catlin, a vital ceremony in the plains Indian life where animals and birds played a prominent part in their beliefs. Episodes of the hunt were re-enacted or pantomimed in a very stylised manner; four singers usually accompanied the performers to the steady, rhythmic beat of drums.

The artist George Catlin spent eight years among the Western Indian tribes, recording their customs and appearance and today his drawings are sometimes the only evidence of many of these vanished tribes. In his portraits he captures the dignity and fierce pride of the Indian before European civilisation intruded into their world.

FAR LEFT Ko-Ko, Mandan girl.
LEFT Black Hawk, Sac Chief
BELOW Wah-Ro-Nee-Sah, Oto Chief

Sacajawea, carrying her son in a papoose, guiding the expedition; reconstruction of a scene by the nineteenth-century artist Alfred Russell.

Soon they were loading the boats. Into the big one went the specimens and all that was to be returned to St Louis, together with the fourteen men who were to go no farther. With them was to go one canoe with two French boatmen who were intending to travel in convoy. Into the two pirogues and the six canoes went the main party which now consisted of thirty-one men, Sacajawea and her infant, who was not quite two months old.

On 7 April at 4 p.m., both parties set out in opposite directions. One, sliding down happily with the current, would be home in a couple of months; the other was striking into the unknown. Meriwether Lewis was not an eloquent man, but what he wrote in his diary that night showed that even he could not fail to be touched by the drama of the moment:

84

This little fleet altho' not quite so rispectable as those of Columbus or Capt. Cook, were still viewed by us with as much pleasure as those deservedly famed adventurers ever beheld theirs; and I dare say with quite as much anxiety for their safety and preservation. we were now about to penetrate a country at least two thousand miles in width, on which the foot of civilized man had never trodden; the good or evil it had in store for us was for experiment yet to determine, and these little vessels contained every article by which we were to expect to subsist or defend ourselves. however, as the state of mind in which we are, generally gives the colouring to events, when the immagination is suffered to wander into futurity, the picture which now presented itself to me was a most pleasing one. entertaining as I do, the most confident hope of succeeding in a voyage which had formed a darling project in my mind for the last ten years, I could but esteem this moment of my departure as among the most happy in my life. The party are in excellent health and sperits, zealously attached to the enterprise, and anxious to proceed; not a whisper or murmur of discontent to be heard among them, but all act in unison, and with the most perfect harmony.

Few explorers already nearly a year out from home could claim as much. And the wonderful thing was that through good times and bad they were to remain a united party.

4   A Land without People

At FIRST IT LOOKED EASY. The Missouri seemed kinder in its upper reaches, although one of the canoes was nearly swamped on the second day. Within a week they had passed the last of the Indian villages and were heading west. If there were no men to be seen, there was plenty of wild life. The buffalo were thick on the prairie land and the beaver were plentiful. The party developed a particular taste for beaver, and Lewis noted in his diary that their favourite food was the liver and tail of this animal. But even in these calm waters there could be sudden panics. Indeed high winds prevented them from travelling on several days, and even though April was half over there was snow in the wind at times, and in the morning they would find ice on the oars and in the kettle. And there was another menace: as the party were camped by the mouth of the Little Muddy river (near where Williston, North Dakota, is today) the party were plagued by clouds of fine white dust that got in their eyes and inflamed them, in their clothes and their food and, what was worse, into the works of the chronometer and the other clocks so that they would not go for more than a few minutes at a time. They were glad to move on from the place. Even the ever-present mosquitoes were not as uncomfortable as this.

The game ashore was as thick as ever: the big-horn sheep were now found as well as deer, buffalo and antelope all grazing together. In the background were the wolves. They did not attack the buffalo *en masse*, but waited until a calf could not keep up with the main herd or a beast stumbled before they went in for the kill. There was plenty for both the hunters and the wolves. As they proceeded they noticed the tracks of a new animal larger than any they had seen before. It was some days before they saw the actual beast, and very formidable it was – their first grizzly bear. For a long time after they came home, Lewis and Clark were thought to have been the first white men ever to have seen one of these great beasts. Certainly they were the first to kill one and describe it closely, if not entirely accurately (Lewis had a theory that the grizzly's testicles were in two separate scrota). In fact, though, grizzlies had been first sighted a century earlier.

Clark and a companion were ashore one day when they spied two grizzlies. Despite Indian warnings that they were very hard to kill, they immediately fired at them. One ran away but the other was wounded and, as the Indians had told them it would,

PREVIOUS PAGES Junction of the Yellowstone and Missouri rivers.

turned on its attackers. Clark and Drewyer, both skilled shots, put ten balls into it before killing it, and even then the bear swam half-way across the river before collapsing finally on a sandbar.

The expedition had no means of weighing the beast, but guessed that it might turn the scale at somewhere between five and six hundred pounds. It stood 8 feet $7\frac{1}{2}$ inches high to the tip of its nose and measured $70\frac{1}{2}$ inches round its chest. It had a 47-inch neck and its claws were $4\frac{3}{8}$ inches long. This first kill had seemed so free from danger that Lewis noted that 'in the hands of skillfull riflemen they are by no means as formidable or dangerous as they have been represented [by the Indians]'. Soon he was to change his tune. On 11 May Bratton, who was suffering badly from boils, and was finding sitting in a canoe unendurably painful, asked permission to walk along the shore. A short while later the river party heard him screaming with terror: he had seen a bear and shot it but failed to kill it. The

White wolves attacking a buffalo isolated from the main herd.

89

Captain Clark and his men shooting Bea

Bears proved very hard to kill, as this illustration from Gass's book shows. The expedition usually relied on mass firing; if the hunters did not have time to reload they had to run for their lives.

bear immediately turned on him before he could reload and chased him along the river bank. Lewis and seven men went ashore and tracked the bear. They killed it with two balls in the skull. Lewis adopted a rather different tone in his diary: 'these bear being so hard to die reather intimedates us all; I must confess that I do not like the gentlemen and had reather fight 2 Indians than one bear.'

Three days later a wounded grizzly nearly put paid to four of the party who, finding the beast lying down, all fired into

it. None of them hit a vital part. The bear was up in a second chasing them and got so close to two of them that they had to throw down their guns and powder-horns and leap down a twenty-foot bank into the river. The bear followed them, but two other hunters who had concealed themselves in bushes managed finally to get in a shot to the brain which killed the bear. Killing grizzlies might be a dangerous business, but it had its compensations. The younger ones provided good meat, and even the toughest old bear could be rendered down to make something like eight gallons of cooking fat of a very superior sort. And, of course, bearskins made warm coverings for the nights which were still cold. Some of the skins were so heavy that it took two men to carry them.

Indeed it was on this part of the trip that the expedition ate more splendidly than at any other time. Their speciality was a white pudding made by Charbonneau. Lewis was sufficiently impressed to record the recipe for what he called 'one of the greatest delicacies of the forest':

About 6 feet of the lower extremity of the large gut of the Buffaloe is the first mossel that the cook makes love to, this he holds fast at one end with the right hand, while with the forefinger and thumb of the left he gently compresses it, and discharges what he says is not good to eat, but of which in the sequel we get a moderate portion; the mustle lying underneath the shoulder blade next to the back, and the fillets are next saught, these are needed up very fine with a good portion of kidney suit; to this composition is added a just proportion of pepper and salt and a small quantity of flour; thus far advanced our skilfull operator. . . . seizes his recepticle, which has never once touched the water, for that would intirely distroy the regular order of the whole procedure; you will not forget that the side you now see is that covered with a good coat of fat provided the anamal be in good order; the operator sceizes the recepticle I say, and tying it fast at one end turns it inward and begins now with repeated evolutions of the hand and arm and a brisk motion of the finger and thumb to put in what he says is *bon pour manger*; thus by stuffing and compressing he soon distends the recepticle to the utmost limmits of it's power of expansion and in the course of it's longditudinal progress it drives from the other end of the recepticle a much larger portion of the [Lewis leaves a blank here, presumably not being able to think of an appropriate word; I leave it to the reader's imagination] than was previously discharged by finger and thumb of the left hand in the former part of the operation; thus when the sides of the recepticle are skilfully exchanged the outer for the iner, and all is compleatly filled with something good to eat, it is tyed at the other end, but not any cut off,

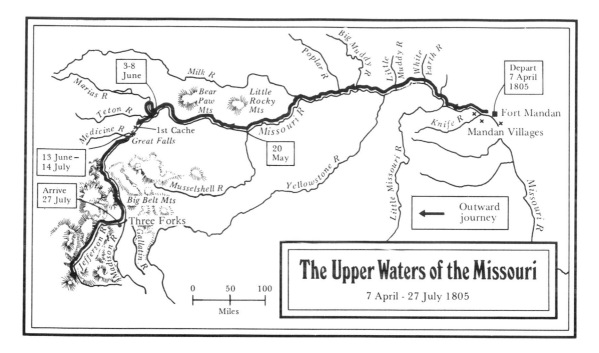

The Upper Waters of the Missouri

7 April - 27 July 1805

for that would make the pattern too scant; it is then baptised in the missouri with two dips and a flirt, and bobbed into the kettle; from whence, after it be well boiled it is taken and fryed in bears oil untill it becomes brown, when it is ready to esswage the pangs of a keen appetite or such as travelers in the wilderness are seldom at a loss for.

Perhaps it tasted good by the banks of the Missouri.

While hunting and paddling occupied most of their attention, they were not ignoring the important business of map-making and surveying. After all, they were now in unknown country. Hitherto there had been no doubt as to which was the course to follow, but now they had come to the point where the Yellowstone river joins the Missouri. It was fortunate that the Indians had told them what to expect here, since there was very little difference between the size of the two rivers as they came together. The Missouri river-bed was measured by Clark as being 520 yards wide with the water occupying 330 yards, while the Yellowstone had a much larger river-bed, 858 yards wide, with 297 yards of water. The right fork, the Missouri, was, however, deeper and faster running. The Yellowstone looked much shallower. They sent Fields up to have a look, and he reported that the other was obviously the main river. In fact if they had taken the left fork they would have reached the lands of the Shoshone much more quickly than by following the Missouri, and it would have proved navigable for their canoes nearly all the way. Indeed it was this route that Clark pioneered on the return journey.

But had they taken this shorter route, they would have missed much of interest and some of their most perilous adventures. They had travelled for about a fortnight after passing the Yellowstone, and were making good progress, when disaster nearly struck. The party was fairly well spread out. The white pirogue – being their largest vessel and the most stable one, had been loaded with all the scientific instruments, books and medicine, most of their trade goods and all their most precious personal possessions – was proceeding merrily under sail. A squall suddenly hit the boat and nearly turned it over. Lewis, who was walking up the far bank of the river with Clark, looked helplessly on while Charbonneau, whom he described as 'the most timid waterman in the world', lost his head and turned the tiller the wrong way. Instead of going head into wind, the boat turned the other way and gybed. Lewis takes up the story:

The wind was so violent that it drew the brace of the squairsail out of the hand of the man who was attending it, and instantly upset the perogue and would have turned her completely topsaturva, had it not been from resistance made by the oarning [awning] against the water. . . . such was their consternation and confusion at this moment, that they suffered the perogue to lie on her side for half a minute before they took the sail in. The perogue then righted but had filled within an inch of the gunwals; Charbonneau still crying to his god for mercy, had not yet recollected the rudder, nor could the repeated orders of the Bowsman, Cruzatte, bring him to his recollection untill he threatened to shot him instantly if he did not take hold of the rudder and do his duty.

Apparently only Cruzatte and Sacajawea kept their heads. While Cruzatte gave directions for the boat to be headed towards the bank and organised the other two men on board to start bailing with a couple of kettles, Sacajawea, with her three-month-old papoose on her back, calmly started collecting all the light articles that were in danger of being washed over the side. After this adventure Lewis and Clark thought it a good idea to give everyone a drink of grog.

The next day was spent in drying the soaked cargo of the pirogue. In the event the damage was not so bad as they

The Lewis and Clark
expedition at the Great Falls
of the Missouri by
O. C. Seltzer.

feared; some of the medicines were spoiled and so was a little gunpowder, and a few small articles had been lost overboard.

The going was beginning to get tougher. The pirogues needed hauling more frequently, sometimes through rapids so fast that the towing crews had to be doubled up. They were leaving the flat prairie lands and entering a hilly area that they thought, wrongly, was the northern end of the Black Hills of Dakota, the southern end of which was already known to the French trappers. Certainly these high, irregularly shaped hills were in much the same line as the Black Hills, but they did not form a continuous chain with the Dakota range. At times the hills came close to the river so that it ran through gorges that were difficult to navigate. The weather did not help; one moment there was fog, the next a dust storm, and later, when they thought that summer must have finally arrived, there was a severe frost and some ice even formed on the river. But Lewis felt repaid for all their struggles when on the afternoon of Sunday, 26 May, he scrambled up one of the hills beside the river and from the top saw a line of snow-capped peaks that he thought were about sixty miles away. It was a moment for reflection. He wrote in his diary:

While I viewed these mountains I felt a secret pleasure in finding myself so near the head of the heretofore conceived boundless Missouri; but when I reflected on the difficulties which this snowey barrier whould most probably throw in my way to the Pacific, and the sufferings and the hardships of myself and party in them, it in some measure conterballanced the joy I had felt in the first moments in which I gazed on them; but as I have always held it a crime to anticipate evils I will believe it a good comfortable road untill I am compelled to believe differently.

In fact, Lewis would be forced to think differently many times before he reached the Pacific. The first thing he had to discover was that these snow-capped mountains he had seen were not the Rockies; they were in fact the Little Rockies, a hundred or so miles to the east of the Rockies proper. Still, the sight of the mountains was enough to spur them on their way. Even at this stage the going was far from smooth. Their hard work poling their boats or hauling them along should have induced sound sleep at nights, but twice there were nocturnal alarms that made subsequent rest difficult. On the first of these occasions the sentry roused the camp when he saw

The grey or 'timber' wolf, who shared with the grizzly a formidable reputation for ferocity; pencil and ink study by W. R. Leigh.

that the campfire had set a nearby tree alight. The camp was hurriedly evacuated, just before a heavy burning branch crashed down on the exact spot where some of the men had been sleeping. A few nights later a buffalo charged their camp-fire. He thundered through the camp, his hooves passing within eighteen inches of the heads of the sleeping men. As they got up, shouting and in some confusion, the animal charged back again but in neither run did it hit anybody.

Much to their surprise they had not seen any Indians; they were convinced some must be around, for there were the relics of lodges and one day they even found a football, but there were no sightings of men. As they passed through one big gorge they saw gruesome evidence that Indians had been around; at the foot of the gorge lay the evil-smelling carcasses of dead buffalo. Lewis and Clark knew what happened, because the people of the Mandan villages had told them of this method of hunting buffalo. A fleet-footed runner was dressed in a hide with a buffalo mask on his head, and lured a herd of the animals towards the top of a steep cliff. He jumped over the edge into a prepared place just below the top where he could lie in safety, while the pursuing herd crashed to their death at the foot of the cliff. It was one of the most wasteful methods of hunting ever invented, and for the runner, one of the most dangerous, for should he not be fast enough or should he slip he would be trampled to death by the charging beasts.

Lewis and Clark were not generally impressed by the country through which they passed, and they made less comment about the actual terrain around them than about almost anything else. Jefferson had not sent them to write a travel agent's prospectus but to make maps and take scientific observations. Every now and again, however, the sheer beauty of their surroundings had to be recorded. For days the boats had been passing between cliffs, and through hills that were growing increasingly high, and on 31 May they suddenly turned a corner to see a place where the cliffs rose two or three hundred feet perpendicularly from the water. The soft sandstone cliffs had been worn away by water until they had been shaped, as Lewis noted, into 'a thousand grotesque figures, which with the help of a little imagination and oblique view, at a distance are made to represent eligant ranges of lofty freestone buildings, having their parapets well stocked with statuary, collumns of various sculpture being grooved and plain, are also seen supporting long galleries in front of these buildings'. Other sections of these remarkable rock formations, incidentally, reminded Prince Maximilian of Wied (who, accompanied by the artist Karl Bodmer, followed Lewis and Clark's trail some thirty years later) of Swiss castles. They seemed to Lewis like ancient classical ruins and pyramids: 'As we passed on it seemed as if these scenes of visionary inchantment would never had an end . . . so perfect are those walls that I should have thought nature had attempted here to rival the human art of masonary had I not recollected that she had first began her work.'

But the next day it was back to a hard grind. The weather was bad with plenty of rain, and the task of towing the boats

This map by Catlin shows the postulated moves of the Mandan Indians whom Catlin believed were the descendants of members of a Welsh expedition under Prince Madoc in the twelfth century, who had mysteriously disappeared. Lewis and Clark also searched for this legendary tribe – without success.

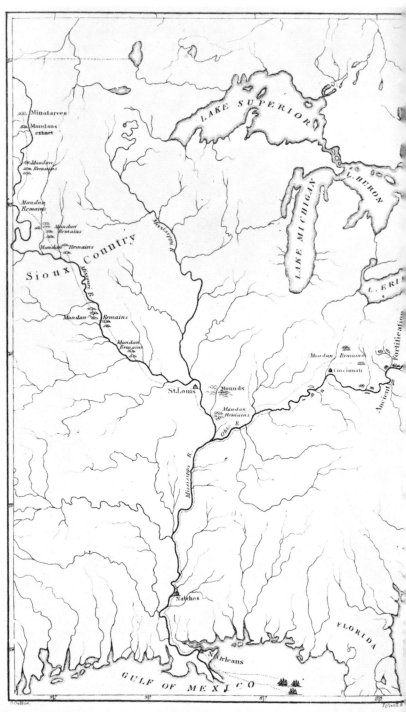

A CHART SHEWING THE MOVES OF THE MANDANS & THE PLACE OF THEIR EXTINCTION.

becamc increasingly difficult. The thick mud or slippery rocks that alternated along the shore made the work terribly difficult, and if they took off their moccasins to get a better purchase they often cut their feet on the sharp stones. A little of the romantic mood must have stayed with them, for Lewis and Clark chose to name the next two rivers they passed not after famous Americans or members of the expedition – most of these had already had at least a creek named after them – but after their girl friends. One river Clark named Judith's river after Miss Julia Hancock, who was later to become his first wife (She was always called Judy; evidently at that time Clark did not know her real name.) Just over a week later Lewis chose the name Maria's river for a stream which he was to explore on the way back, without Clark. He was never, however, fated to marry Miss Maria Wood. It seems that he had worshipped her from afar, and had left on the expedition without declaring his love. She was later to become a Mrs Clarkson.

But which was to be Maria's river? The expedition had arrived at a fork, and the information that the Indians had given them at Fort Mandan did not enable them to decide which was the proper way. (In fact the Indians had told them about two routes to the Continental Divide, but they had

The Swiss artist Karl Bodmer accompanied a German prince, Maximilian of Wied, on his route into the interior in 1833–4 and recorded his impressions of their travels. ABOVE Meeting with Minataree Indians.

OVERLEAF The extraordinary rock formations bordering the Upper Missouri, in which Bodmer found a resemblance to Swiss castles, clearly seen in this lithograph.

Dean Cornwall's impression of Lewis and Clark and their companions high up the Missouri river. Lewis holds the octant, Clark the map. Artistic licence allows Indians to be present.

thought they were being told about only one; the result was that at various times they were rather confused in trying to sort out which way to turn.) Both forks of the river looked equally possible. It was 3 June by now, and they could not afford to lose time by taking the wrong fork. They must contact the Shoshone and hire horses to cross the Rockies. Otherwise they were in danger of being caught by the winter snows on the high slopes, where they would have no chance of survival. Lewis and Clark made camp at the point where the rivers joined. Each set off up one of the rivers with a scouting party, agreeing to meet again five days later to compare notes on their respective journeys.

On the face of it Lewis's river looked the most possible; it ran west while Clark's turned due south, but neither was certain. The weather continued to be extremely bad, and after two days Lewis, confident that his river was going too far to the north, turned for home. To get back to camp quickly, the party tried to take a short cut across the top of the bluffs. It was far more dangerous than they thought, and after a few yards Lewis found himself slipping towards a ninety-foot precipice. He managed to save himself by driving his short hunting spear, called an espontoon, into the earth and getting a purchase on that. A few minutes later, hearing a cry, he found that one of his party, Windsor, had slipped and was lying flat with his right arm and leg overhanging the precipice, while he held on as best he could with his left hand. Like a true commander Lewis, as he recorded later, 'disguised my feelings and spoke very calmly to him and assured him he was in no kind of danger, to take the knife out of his belt behind him with his wright hand and dig a hole in the face of the bank to receive his wright foot which he did and then raised himself to his knees'. After some exploratory clutching he was able to make his way to safety, but Lewis had had enough. He ordered the party down to the river bank and they made their way back to camp through mud or, where the banks were impassable, by wading, sometimes up to their waists in water.

Clark's party had an easier time, though Fields was chased up a tree by a bear which prowled round its base until the rest of the party drove it away. The southern fork ran fairly fast through narrow gorges, and the going was far from easy. There was even some snow in the rain, and it was a weary and sore-footed party that returned to base camp.

Like the sensible men that they were, Lewis and Clark consulted the boatmen among their party about which route to choose. Cruzatte, the senior boatman, was quite convinced that the north fork (the one Lewis had prospected) was the right one, and his fellow boatmen agreed; but they were overruled. Lewis and Clark had both independently come to the conclusion that the south fork was the correct one, and the disciplined party immediately accepted their decision. However, they agreed to leave one of the pirogues at this point and to make a cache of provisions and medicine, so that there would be something to return to if it proved that they had taken the wrong fork.

This was the first of several caches that they were to make in the next part of their journey. A cache was a hole scooped out of the ground with a narrow opening, about twenty inches across. For the first foot of its depth it kept to this diameter, and was then dug out sideways in the shape of kettle or an old-fashioned leather bottle, so that a quantity of stores could

be hidden inside without the ground appearing to have been
disturbed. The earth excavated from the hole was put carefully on a blanket so that the surrounding ground should not be
marked. When completed, this cache was about six feet deep
with a floor of sticks. The goods were carefully piled in, leaving
a gap between the goods and the walls, so that they would not
get damp. Sticks were laid on top of the supplies and the earth
was shovelled in and painstakingly smoothed down across
the narrow opening. No obvious sign was left of the position of
the cache, but careful sightings were made so that it could be
discovered later. The red pirogue was hidden in thick undergrowth on an island in the river.

Lewis, having named the north fork Maria's river, set off
across country with four men to scout ahead while Clark
brought the main party by water. As this was the last time that
they would be together for a while, they had what they called
'a frolic'; they danced to the fiddle and had a drink all round.
At least they were alive and still heading on into the wilderness.
Suddenly things seemed to be taking a turn for the better. It
seemed like an omen when Lewis's party, for the only time on
the trip, killed two bears with one shot apiece. Even when the
leader had a sudden attack of dysentery and found that he had
no medicine with him, he experimented with boiling the twigs
of the choke-cherry tree and drinking the resultant infusion,
and felt better the next day. Two days later Lewis was walking
ahead, slightly worried that he was on the wrong route,
because the river was still turning south. Suddenly he saw what
looked like a column of smoke in the air and heard a great
roaring sound. This could be nothing but the spray and the
crash of the great falls of the Missouri, the first of a series of five
that Lewis was the first white man to see.

The river was three hundred yards wide here. Sometimes the
water fell free for a hundred feet or more, and at others it
cascaded in white foam over broken rocks for as much as two
hundred yards at a time. Lewis wrote in his diary:

. . . from the reflection of the sun on the sprey or mist which arrises
from these falls there is a beautifull rainbow produced which adds
not a little to the beauty of the majestically grand scenery, after
wrighting this imperfect idea which it conveyed of the scene that I
determined to draw my pen through it and start again, but then
reflected that I could not perhaps succeed better than pening the
first impressions of the mind.

106

It is easy to sympathise with Lewis wishing that he had the pencil of a Titian or the pen of the poet Thompson. At least he was lucky to see the falls in their full majesty. Now, inevitably, they have been shaped and harnessed to do their duty as part of a hydroelectric plant.

All in all Lewis was having an adventurous time. The next day he pressed on along the side of the river with the falls thundering beside him, and above them he found a vista opening out in front of him of a beautiful plain heavily populated with game. He picked out a buffalo and shot it through the lungs. As he stood waiting for it to drop, so certain that he had killed that he did not bother to reload his gun, he suddenly realised that a huge bear was charging at him. He had not time now to reload, and took to his heels. After eighty yards, with the bear gaining on him steadily, he reached the river and leapt in. The bear hesitated and looked as if it was about to jump in also. Lewis, with only his hunting spear in his hand, thought that this was the end for him, but suddenly the bear took fright and lumbered off. This was not all, for later in the day as Lewis made his way wearily back to his companions he was charged by three buffaloes. He had to take to his heels again. This time he had to run across a thick carpet of prickly pear, the cactus-like fruit that grows very close to the ground and is armed with long sharp spikes that go straight through the soles of moccasins. During the next few weeks this was one of the great discomforts that the expedition had to face, even though they doubled the soles of their moccasins. Every night they had to examine their feet and pick out as many as sixty thorns from them.

Lewis sent Fields back with a message that they had surveyed the extent of the falls and that Clark and those with him should take the boats as far as they could and then make camp, ready to carry the boats and supplies overland to a point where they could launch them again above the rough water. Lewis followed the next day and found that Clark had reached the furthest point he could with the boats and had made camp. He had also been forced to stop because Sacajawea was very ill. She was obviously paying the penalty for so much exertion so soon after the birth of her child. They tried what medicines they had on her, and for three days they feared that she might die. Then quite suddenly, after they had given her a drink from a nearby sulphur spring, she began to improve and was soon eating grilled buffalo, well seasoned with salt and pepper, and sucking

'Chasing off the Grizzlies'
by Karl Bodmer.

down meat broth. A couple of days later she made Lewis furious by eating unripe fruit and making herself ill again. However, she soon recovered.

A reconnaissance showed that they would have to make a land crossing of about eighteen miles over fairly rough country, with a lot of prickly pear. Clark went ahead to mark out the best route, while six men stayed behind to fashion wheels for a rough cart they intended to make for hauling the canoes and supplies. Once again the expedition's luck was in, for close to the camp was a cottonwood tree with a trunk twenty-two inches wide. It was the only suitable wood for miles around for making wheels. Even this gave them some trouble, for the wood tended to splinter and the carpenters had to have several tries before they succeeded in completing a pair of wheels. These they fitted on each end of the mast of the remaining pirogue, which they intended to leave behind here with a second cache of heavy equipment. For the next week they worked hard at 'portaging' the equipment and stores over to the far side of the falls, and making more wheels and axles as the first attempts broke. Several of the men collapsed from over-work but recovered after a rest.

At the far end of the route, a party was set to work constructing Lewis's special secret device. It had travelled all the way with them in a packing case. During the winter when they had been waiting to start, he had been to Harper's Ferry and had blacksmiths there make him the iron framework for a thirty-five-foot-long boat, which they could construct when they had been forced to abandon their conventional boats. All that was needed was a covering of skins, and they had plenty of these. They even managed to find suitable wood for internal fittings. All the parts of the boat were there except one screw, which was missing; Fields managed to contrive a substitute for it. Soon the elk skins were stretched over the framework and sewn together. The only trouble was that they needed pitch to make the seams watertight. They dug holes hopefully to look for tar but could not find any, so in the end they compromised on a mixture of powdered charcoal and beeswax. It looked fine and seemed to set well when they slung the boat up over fires to dry it out. Finally came the day for launching. When they put the boat on the water it bounced like a cork. Here was just the light boat they needed for the shallow waters of the uppermost reaches of the Missouri. But as the day wore on, the boat began to settle and fill with water. The artificial 'pitch' was useless, and all the seams were pouring water. Sadly Lewis abandoned his brainchild and sent off a party to look for trees to make conventional canoes. They had to go eight miles to find suitable trees, and it took an extra week to make them. It is perhaps a sign of Clark's great tact and of the wonderful understanding between the two commanders that while Lewis comments sadly in his diary about the failure of his 'experiment', Clark passes it over in silence.

To add to their troubles, the weather broke. For several days it was hot and sticky and there were thunderstorms. One day the men were working almost naked because of the heat when a black cloud came out of the west, bringing a hailstorm so fierce that most of the party were bruised by the stones and one man was knocked down three times. For Clark, it was nearly the end of the journey. He discovered that he had left some notes behind and went back to look for them; York, Charbonneau, and Sacajawea and her baby went along for the exercise. They were ambling along the bank of the river when the storm broke and they found shelter in a narrow ravine. Suddenly Clark saw a torrent of water pouring down the ravine towards them. He shouted at them to jump clear and pushed Sacajawea, who was clutching her baby in her arms, up the rock face in front of him. Charbonneau, who was paralysed with fear, only just got clear, losing his gun and ammunition pouch (a terrible crime). But he was not the only person to lose something: Clark found that his compass and his umbrella had been carried away. This is, by the way, the only mention of an umbrella on the trip. It seems strangely incongruous that these frontiersmen in their buckskins and moccasins should have had with them such a recently invented fad of fashion as an umbrella.

Another Independence Day had come around, but beyond a sharing out of the last of the spirits, except for a small quantity kept strictly for medicinal use only, and a dance in the evening, there was no celebration. Ten days later the canoes were finished, and the following morning the expedition set off again on the calm and inviting waters above the falls, the river banks carpeted with flowers. But as they went on they realised that, beautiful though the scenery might be with the high hills pressing down on the river, they were passing out of the buffaloes' pastures and soon, unless they contacted the Shoshone, they would be short of food.

The rest of July passed without any notable incident beyond the normal troubles in making their way up rapids, sometimes so turbulent that the canoes had to be carried, sometimes easy enough to be tackled by double-manned canoes paddling hard with the help of a towing-party ashore. On 22 July, when they were some 166 miles above the falls, they were heartened by Sacajawea's saying that she recognised the country; they were not far from the Three Forks of the Missouri, where they should meet her people. Clark and three others set out on a scouting trip. Climbing over a high hill, they found a broad 'Indian road', a clearly defined track, which they followed for a

Sacajawea pointing out her homeland to Lewis and Clark at Three Forks of the Missouri. Very much an artist's impression; it is unlikely that the explorers were so clean and tidy.

long way without seeing anyone. The going was tough, with a lot of prickly pear, so they abandoned their footslogging and made their way back to the river to rejoin the rest of the party. As they must be nearing Indians, the commanders hoisted flags in their canoes to show they were white men and pressed on. Every time they climbed a hill, they could see big mountains, shining and snow-capped, to the west of them. Without Indian help they would never be able to find the passes.

Again Clark went ahead to reconnoitre, and on 25 July he reached the Three Forks. There was no obvious indication

which one he should take, so he tried the northernmost one first
because he saw beside it the marks of a horse's hooves. On
the face of it, however, this fork, which they later named the
Jefferson river, did not look a very promising route.

The strain of travelling in the heat was beginning to tell.
First Charbonneau collapsed and then Fields. Clark sent them
back to Three Forks to make camp while he and York climbed
a nearby mountain to see if they could find any clue as to which
fork to take. There was no clear indication, though they did
see some burned prairie land that the Indians had obviously

set on fire for some purpose. Clark now began to feel unwell – bilious, with a high temperature and aching bones – and dragged himself back to the camp, where the others, now convalescent, built a shelter to shade him from the heat. When Lewis and the canoe party caught them up Clark was still very sick, so they decided to make camp for a couple of days. Then Lewis would set off by land 'to find these yellow gentlemen', again following the Jefferson river. The other two forks clearly ran too far to the south to be worth investigating. They decided that as the river broke into three apparently equal streams it would be wrong to call any one of them the Missouri, so the other two were called the Madison and the Gallatin after members of Jefferson's cabinet.

Lewis, Charbonneau, Gass and Drewyer set off up the Jefferson while Clark and his party loaded the canoes again and followed. The going by foot was much easier than by water, as the fast-flowing river rushed down from the mountains in a constant succession of rapids. Once a canoe was upset and Whitehouse was thrown into the water. Had it been only a few inches shallower he would have been crushed into the sharp rocks of the river-bed as the boat passed over him, but he escaped with a fright. They came to a fork in the river, but could not find the sign which Lewis had promised to leave to show them which way to take. (They later found that a beaver had chopped down the tree on which the message had been fixed.) Fortunately Drewyer turned up soon after, bringing in some game he had killed, and put them on the right track. Shannon was also out hunting and got lost again. It was three days this time before he turned up again. The one thing that cheered them, as they dried the baggage after the soaking it had got in a bad rapid, was that above them towered a strangely shaped rock like a beaver's head. This rock Sacajawea positively identified as being close to the Shoshone summer camping-grounds.

Lewis, who had come back to see if the main party was all right, immediately decided to set off again, this time taking Drewyer, Shields and McNeill with him. Not far up the river they found another Indian road and followed it, looking for freshly made traces of horses' hooves. They found some, but they soon petered out. It looked as if they had gone up a false trail, so they went back to where the road seemed to have forked and followed the other track. It did not look very hope-

ful, but Lewis was determined to go on. To make sure that they would not miss any possible sign of Indian activity, he made Shields wade across the river to go up the other bank. The mountains stood farther back here, and they were going along meadows on either side. The river was only a tiny stream now. Since they had reached the highest point that the canoes would be able to go, they left a note for Clark to camp at this point. They plodded on; as always, there seemed no sign of life on the rolling plain in front of them. Then suddenly some two miles ahead they saw a man on horseback heading towards them.

Beavers were in great demand in the early years of the nineteenth century when their pelts were used for making top hats. It was the search for these animals that first brought trappers into the North West.

5   To the Mountains

LEWIS WAS BY HIMSELF, with Shields and Drewyer about a hundred yards on each side of him. McNeill had stayed behind to guard the camp. As Lewis reached into his pack for his telescope the Indian was still riding towards him, seemingly unconcerned. Through the telescope Lewis could see that the horseman, bow and arrow on his back, was riding without stirrups, and wearing a robe with a fur collar. He was different from any Indian that Lewis had seen before, shorter and of a darker complexion than the Mandans, and in his hair he wore golden-eagle feathers and something that glittered in the sun (it was, he discovered later, fragments of mother-of-pearl). Slowly Lewis and the Indian closed the gap between them. The Minnetarees that he had spoken to during the winter had told him that the sign for peace was to wave a blanket in the air and then spread it out on the ground three times. He did this, and as a further sign of good intentions laid down his rifle. The Indian was obviously worried by the presence of the two men on either side of Lewis, but their commander did not dare shout to them to stand still for fear of frightening the Indian. Lewis advanced a little and then paused again to take some beads and other trade goods out of his pack. Holding them out, he shouted 'Tab-ba-bone', the word Sacajawea had told him was the Shoshone for 'white man'. As Lewis closed to a hundred paces, the Indian wheeled his horse round, but he still did not move, looking suspiciously over his shoulder. Lewis now rolled up his sleeve to show his white skin. As he recorded in his diary, he thought that the hot summer had tanned his face and hands as dark as any Indian. At the same time he made a frantic signal to Shields and Drewyer to stand still. Drewyer froze, but Shields still went on closing in from the side. The Indian took one more frightened look and then whipped up his horse, leapt over a stream and disappeared into the brushwood. After Lewis had said a few words to Shields, who claimed that he had not seen the signal, the three men gave chase and followed the hoof-marks for a few miles. A heavy hailstorm forced them to stop to take shelter. When it passed they found that the rain had revived the grass and removed the traces of the horse's passage. Sadly they returned to camp.

Their stocks of food were running low. The next morning they breakfasted off the last of their venison, which left them with only about a pound of bacon and a small sack of flour.

PREVIOUS PAGES Lewis, Clark and Sacajawea; sculpture by Henry Lion.

118

They set out hopefully. Once again they saw Indians, this time a man and several women accompanied by some dogs. As the first one had done, they stood uncertain while Lewis went towards them making signs of friendship and holding out trade goods. He had no better luck this time: the Indians ran away, but some of their dogs came quite close to Lewis. He had the somewhat frenzied idea of tying beads in a handkerchief round a dog's neck in the hope that it would return to its owners and lead them back to Lewis. After chasing them around a bit, he gave up; the dogs were not going to be caught, and eventually they ran off.

Once again the party pressed on, following the Jefferson

Indians discovering Lewis and Clark; painting by Charles M. Russell.

our rout lay along the ridge of a high mountain
course S 20. W. — 18. me. used the snow for cooking.

Thursday September 19th 1805.

Set out this morning a little after sunrise an
continued our rout about the same course of yesterday
or S. 20. W. for 6 miles when the ridge terminated and
we to our inexpressable joy discovered a large
tract of Prairie country lying to the S. W. and widen
-ing as it appeared to extend to the W. through that
plain the Indian informed us that the Columbia
river, (in which we were in surch) run. this plain
appeared to be about 60. Miles distant, but our guide
assured us that we should reach its borders tomorro
the appearance of this country, our only hope for
subsistance greately revived the sperits of the party
already reduced and much weakend for the want of
food. — the country is thickly covered with a very

Extract from Meriwether
Lewis's diary recording the
crossing of the Continental
Divide on 19 September 1805.

river, which had now become a tiny stream. Indeed, just before
it disappeared into the mountainside, McNeill straddled it
and shouted that he never thought he would bestride the mighty
Missouri, of which the Jefferson was the extreme point. As
they crossed the ridge, they found another stream flowing
down the mountainside, going westwards. Almost without
knowing it they had crossed the Continental Divide. Was this
little stream the beginning of the mighty Columbia river? It
might be; and in a sense it was, since this was the source of the
Lemhi river, the water from which ran into the Salmon river,
from it into the Snake, and then finally into the Columbia.
But, more important, as they stood on the ridge – it was

actually the Lemhi Pass, where now the states of Montana and Idaho join – they realised that this was going to be no easy glide down the river to the sea. Between them and the Pacific, as they could now see, stood range after range of snow-capped mountains, higher than any they had seen so far.

Another night came, and the last of the bacon was eaten. There was no sign of game in the rocky hills and steep valleys where they now found themselves. They could only follow the Indian road and hope for the best. This morning it looked as though their luck had changed, for quite early in the day they saw another party only a hundred yards away. In the pattern that had now grown familiar, the man and the women with him would not wait for the explorers to catch up with them, but ran away. A couple of hours later, though, coming round a corner of rock, Lewis and his companions suddenly discovered themselves within thirty paces of a party of four Indian women. The two young ones immediately disappeared into the undergrowth but an old woman and a twelve-year-old child, realising that they could not escape, knelt down and bowed their heads forward in submission, expecting that the wild shouting figures that had appeared would immediately execute them. Much to their surprise the 'attackers' came up slowly, spoke gently in a strange tongue and lifted the old woman to her feet.

One of the party – it was Drewyer – spoke to her by signs and asked her to call the other women who had hidden themselves. When they came out, Lewis, a striking figure in buckskins and a cocked hat with a feather in it, bared his arm to show he was white. Then he reached into his pack and brought out some blue beads and a pewter looking-glass which he offered them as presents. As the women stood admiring themselves and their gifts, there came the sound of a large party on horseback arriving. In a moment or two some sixty horsemen, all armed with bows and arrows and some of them carrying war clubs and wearing leather armour, came into sight. The Indian the explorers had seen first that morning had run back to camp, and this was a rescue party. Lewis immediately threw down his gun and ordered his companions to do the same. Slowly they advanced towards the man who was obviously the chief. He was watching them most suspiciously. It was a nasty moment, but one of the women saved the situation. She broke away from the group and ran towards the chief, showing him the presents that Lewis had given her. The tension

Shoshone woman catching a
horse; painting by
Alfred J. Miller.

relaxed when the woman came close to the chief and he saw that Lewis had daubed her cheek with vermilion paint, which he had been assured by the Mandans was a sign of peace among the Shoshone.

The chief – they were to discover that his name was Cameahwait ('He who never walks') – dismounted, came forward, put his left arm over Lewis's right shoulder and hugged him, rubbing his cheeks against Lewis's. Two of his companions did the same thing, leaving Lewis feeling slightly sticky from the grease and paint that had rubbed off from their faces on to his. It was up to Lewis to make the next move, so he called on his companions to get out the ceremonial pipe they carried and to light up. They all sat in a circle, the Shoshone taking off their moccasins as a sign of courtesy. As they could not converse directly, they had to rely on sign language, but they were able to establish that the explorers had come in peace and represented the majesty of the Great Father. For their part the Indians explained that they had been frightened that the white men – they had never seen one before – were a party of their traditional enemies the Minnetarees of Fort de Prairie who had earlier in the year killed twenty of their warriors, stolen many of their horses and destroyed all but one of their leather lodges.

The party now moved to the Shoshone encampment, which consisted of about a couple of hundred people with several hundred horses grazing round their willow huts. The visitors were ushered to the only remaining leather lodge where the ground was strewn with green willow branches, covered with a buffalo robe. It was now time for more ceremonial greetings. Cameahwait and some of his companions made long speeches and undertook complicated rituals with their pipes, pointing the bowls to the four main points of the compass. Lewis distributed the remainder of the trade goods that they had brought with them among the women and children. (The formal presentation of medals would have to wait until Clark arrived with the baggage.) The Indians, for their part, explained that they were very short of food. In the summer months they withdrew into these valleys for safety and lived mostly on berries and roots, while in the colder weather they came out on to the upper reaches of the Missouri to hunt on the prairies after the hostile tribes had withdrawn to their winter quarters. However, they gave the visitors some cakes

made out of dried berries and choke-cherries. Then the
Indians started to dance. After several hours, Lewis slipped
away to his lodge but on the way an Indian stopped him and
pressed into his hand a small piece of boiled salmon. Apart
from the pleasure of eating it, he guessed that it must have
come from a river that emptied itself into the Pacific: he was
within reach of his goal.

After so many delays and disappointments, he was able to
record in his diary for this momentous day, Tuesday, 13
August:

This evening the Indians entertained us with their dancing nearly
all night. at 12 O'Ck I grew sleepy and retired to rest leaving the men
to amuse themselves with the Indians. I observe no essential difference
between the music and manner of dancing among this nation and
those of the Missouri. I was several times awoke in the course of the
night by their yells but was too much fortiegued to be deprived of a
tolerable sound night's repose.

125

The next couple of days were thoroughly frustrating, not only because of the exhausting and at times confusing business of conducting all conversations in sign language, but because the Shoshone were continually changing their minds. Lewis explained to Cameahwait that he wanted a party of Indians on horseback to come with him to meet the rest of the expedition and to carry their main stores to camp. At first this was all happily agreed, but then suddenly the Indians changed their mind. After much prodding, Cameahwait explained that some of his councillors were convinced that Lewis and his companions were agents for the Minnetarees and were luring them all into a trap. Lewis insisted that this was not so, but the stalemate might have persisted if Drewyer had not been successful in shooting an antelope from a borrowed horse. The Indians with him on this trip crowded round the carcass and ate most of the entrails raw on the spot. This hunting success somewhat reassured them. In addition, Lewis gave instructions for half their flour to be used in cooking a sort of pudding flavoured with local berries which he shared with Cameahwait and some of his friends.

Eventually the Indians agreed to go to Three Forks to meet the canoe party. Indeed all the men insisted on coming, and some of the women as well, while those who stayed behind set up a terrible howl, as Lewis recorded in his diary, 'imploring the great sperit to protect their warriors as if they were going to certain destruction'. It was a far from comfortable journey for Lewis, who was at first given a ride on a horse behind one of the Indians, but found riding without saddle or stirrups so unpleasant that he preferred to walk. Drewyer killed a deer, and once again the greater part of it was immediately eaten raw, though he reserved a quarter for Lewis and the other two who cooked their ration. During the day several other deer were killed and eaten and all seemed to be going well, but when the party arrived at the point where Lewis expected Clark to be waiting for him, there was no sign of the boats. All the old suspicions were aroused. Lewis was now in a quandary; he could not afford to lose the Indians. If they left now they might make off into some inaccessible valley, and he would never be able to get the horses he must have to cross the mountains. There was only one thing to do: he handed his rifle over to the chief as a sign of complete confidence, showing by signs that if the chief thought Lewis an enemy he might shoot him at any time he wanted to. This seemed to work, but Lewis decided to try a bit of trickery. He knew that just down the river there was a stick in which he had left a note for Clark. He told Drewyer to fetch it, making sure that an Indian – none of the white men ever moved without a 'spy' dogging his footsteps – noticed him take it from the stick. Drewyer brought it back to Lewis, who read it in front of Cameahwait and announced to him by signs that this was a message from his 'brother' and that he would soon be coming. Lewis radiated as much confidence as he could, but he was worried: 'I slept but little as might be well expected, my mind dwelling on the state of the expedition which I have ever held in equal estimation with my own existence, and the fait of which appeared at this moment to depend in a great measure upon the caprice of a few savages who are ever as fickle as the wind.'

The next morning, needless to say, he was up early and at first light sent Drewyer on a scouting expedition down the river. Again he was shadowed by an Indian. He had not gone far before, on turning a corner, he saw Clark walking up the bank with Charbonneau and Sacajawea. The Indian immediately returned to camp to report, but all Cameahwait's old suspicions returned and he insisted that Lewis and his companions must wear Shoshone fur tippets round their necks so that they would look for all the world like Indians. In return Lewis gave his cocked hat with a feather to Cameahwait to wear. Would the Indians panic? Or, indeed, would Clark? He, after all, had only two companions and there in the distance was a large body of Indians and no obvious sign of Lewis. It was Sacajawea who saved the situation. She started sucking her fingers, her sign to Clark that the approaching Indians belonged to her tribe. She danced forward, and almost at the same moment Clark realised that the leading 'Indian' running towards them was Drewyer. Clark decided to wait until the boat party caught up – they were only just behind around a bend in the river – and they then all went to the camp. The main group was late because the going up the Jefferson had been much harder than either of the leaders reckoned, and they had been fighting against rapids most of the time. Indeed, Clark's party was nearer to mutiny than at any other time. They had not had the excitement of going on ahead scouting for signs of the Indians, just the daily grind of paddling and towing up a river that never seemed to end.

Sacajawea's meeting with her relatives of the Shoshone tribe; Lewis stands in the foreground: painting by Charles M. Russell.

As they came to the camp one of the Indian women rushed at Sacajawea and they embraced each other, both bursting into floods of tears. It turned out that this woman had been captured at the same time as Sacajawea but had escaped some months later. Both thought the other dead. There was also a surprise in store for the expedition when Sacajawea came forward and embraced Cameahwait. They had always been a little sceptical about her claim to be of Shoshone royal blood, but she was in fact the sister of the chief and was welcomed as such. He told her that all their family had been killed except himself, one brother who was away hunting and a nephew, the son of their elder sister, whom Sacajawea promptly adopted for the dura-

tion of her stay with her people. There was one slight complication that emerged during the next few days: this was that by Shoshone custom Sacajawea had been contracted in marriage when she was a child. Technically her husband, who was present, could claim her and put her to work in the camp. However, and fortunately, when he saw that she had borne another man's child he agreed to relinquish her.

These personal troubles over, and the interpreters having arrived, the leaders could settle down to discussions with the Indians. Now that the main supplies had arrived Lewis could give the proper gifts to the chiefs – medals, uniform coats as well as beads, and knives and tobacco. The knives were

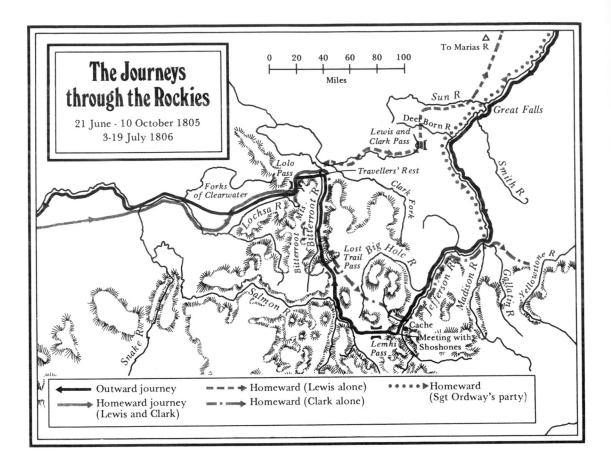

The Journeys
through the Rockies

21 June - 10 October 1805
3-19 July 1806

To Marias R

Sun R

Great Falls

Dee Born R

Lewis and
Clark Pass

Smith R

Lolo
Pass

Travellers' Rest

Forks
of Clearwater

Clark
Fork

Lochsa R

Bitterroot Mts.
Bitterroot R

Lost
Trail
Pass

Big Hole R

Salmon R

Jefferson R

Madison R

Gallatin R

Yellowstone R

Snake R

Cache

Meeting with
Shoshones

Lemhi
Pass

0   20   40   60   80   100
Miles

→ Outward journey
→ Homeward journey
(Lewis and Clark)
⇢ Homeward (Lewis alone)
⇢ Homeward (Clark alone)
•••• Homeward
(Sgt Ordway's party)

particularly welcome, for not only were Lewis and Clark the
first white men the Indians had seen but the Shoshone's contact
with any Europeans was much less than any other tribe the
expedition had come across. They had one or two Spanish
axes which had passed through the hands of numerous tribes
on their way to the Shoshone, but the cutting-tools they
generally used were made of flint. Lewis made his usual
speech about the protective arm of the White Father being
placed round the shoulders of obedient Indians and the benefits
that would arise from trading with the United States and the
United States alone. In return he asked for information. They
had crossed the Continental Divide and they really did not
know which way to turn. Cameahwait produced an old Indian
who claimed that he knew all about the lands that lay to the
south-west. He gave them a long rambling account from which
they got the impression that the rivers that ran in that direction

130

ended up in the Colorado and ran down into the Gulf of California. He also made a number of rather wild statements about the shape of the mountains which also proved, long after Lewis and Clark's time, to be inaccurate.

Lewis and Clark were still convinced that the best way to travel was by river, and they wanted to get to the Columbia as soon as possible. While these talks were going on, in fact, Clark went off to look for suitable trees to make canoes. He found none, and his first reconnaissance trip suggested that it was unlikely that they would find a navigable river within easy reach of their present camp. They would have to buy horses and find a guide to take them over what looked very difficult mountains.

Cameahwait was able to produce another old Indian whom the expedition called Toby, who knew the land to the north of the camp. He told them the route that the Nez Percé Indians, a Columbian river people, used to make their way through the mountains on their visits to the upper reaches of the Missouri. After several days of discussion – Lewis noted in his diary that you must never press the Indians for too much information at one time; they easily became fatigued – it became clear that they would not be able to proceed without a guide. After much bargaining, Toby agreed to go with them. Cameahwait was proving difficult over the sale of horses. He said that a great many of his had been taken by the Minnetarecs and he had none to spare. Charbonneau and Sacajawea were sent off to negotiate with another branch of the Shoshones who might have some. Lewis was convinced that they could not proceed without at least twenty-five.

Clark went off once again on a prospecting mission. The best way seemed to him to be to go north-west and then follow the Salmon river through the mountains, but after he had travelled seventy miles, accompanied by Toby, it became obvious that the party could not possibly get themselves or their baggage across the precipitous mountains; and the Salmon river at this point was a torrent on which no boat could live. After consulting with his guide, he decided to make camp and wait for Lewis, since the north route to the Snake river was the only possible one. Meanwhile Lewis was faced with a problem. The Shoshone were the most pleasant Indians that they had met so far; they were very obliging, the women mending their visitors' moccasins and looking after them well, but they certainly could not be trusted with the supplies that the expedition would be forced to abandon at this point. Not only would Lewis and his men have to construct a cache but they would have to do it without the Indians seeing what they were up to. This meant that small parties had to creep out of the camp at night, do their excavating and be back in their sleeping quarters before the Indians were awake in the morning. This took several days. The canoes, which were of no use to the Shoshones, who did not travel by water, were filled with stones and sunk to the bottom of the river; the Indians promised to see that they came to no harm.

The problem of the horses was still not solved. Charbonneau had managed to obtain a few, and Cameahwait arranged for the hire of a couple of mules, which proved more costly - two axes, two knives and some paint for each – than horses; but even so they could muster only nine animals. Most of the time relations with the Shoshone remained friendly, but there was some friction: the Indians did not seem to bother to hunt for themselves while the explorers could do it for them, and this led to arguments. On one occasion Drewyer was out hunting and spent the night with some Indians. In the morning a young brave stole his rifle. Drewyer chased after him, but would not have caught him if the young man had not been slowed down by his squaws who were riding with him. Drewyer caught the women and made them shout to the thief that he must return the gun or there would be trouble. He shouted back that he needed the rifle to fight his enemies, but Drewyer, by distracting his attention, got close enough to grab hold of the gun and try to wrest it from him. The Indian, realising that he was losing the struggle, let go of the gun and galloped away. In reprisal Drewyer seized the buffalo robes and food the young man left behind.

On another occasion Lewis had to speak firmly to Cameahwait about his refusal to let them have any more horses. The chief agreed to hand some over, but Lewis could never be certain that he would not change his mind again. The price seemed to be going up, too. One horse, of a better quality than some of the others which had sores on their backs, cost a pistol, powder, a hundred balls and a knife. Eventually after more than a week of bargaining the party managed to obtain twenty-nine beasts. Primarily they were for carrying goods, but it was expected that they would also be needed for casualties

Distant view of the Rocky Mountains.

in the mountains ahead; those who were unable to walk would have to ride. In addition, the Indians had told them that there were no buffalo west of the Bitter Root Mountains, the chain that they had to cross to reach the Columbia river, so their stock of horses also represented their reserve food supplies.

Although it was only late August, the weather at night was getting very cold. There was frost on the ground in the mornings, and it was essential for them to get a move on if they were not to be caught by the snow in the high passes. At last Cameahwait was ready to move, and the last days of August were spent in the slow march down the Lemhi river and up one of the forks of the Salmon river that would take them north to where they hoped they might cross the mountains. After a while the Shoshone would leave them to go to their winter hunting-grounds. This happened on 2 September, and only Toby and his son were left to guide the explorers.

A couple of days earlier Clark had rejoined the main party, full of stories of the friendliness of the Indians who lived hidden in this tough, rocky country. At first these isolated groups had been terrified by the arrival of white men, but when they discovered the explorers' friendliness they had been happy to share what little food they had, mostly fish and berries, with Clark's party. Lewis in his turn had an incredible event to report. During their journey with the Shoshone, he had noticed one of the Indian women get off her horse and sit down beside a creek. As the party continued on its way, he saw that one of the women stayed with her. He asked Cameahwait what was happening, and the chief told him that the woman was giving birth to a child. To Lewis's astonishment, an hour later the two women caught up with the cavalcade, the mother carrying her child in her arms and seeming to be in perfect health.

Soon there was no more time for stories, as the country they were now entering was by far the hardest going they had yet encountered. There was no discernible trail, and they had to make their way over sharp rocks and cut their way through undergrowth. Finally the mountains closed in on the creek sides entirely and the party had to make their way as best they could up the precipitous hillside to seek out better going. Several of the horses fell, some of them narrowly escaping

Lewis and Clark meeting
Flathead Indians at Ross's
Hole. Lewis and Clark are
on the right, Sacajawea is
seated on the ground and
York stands by the horses.

from toppling down the mountainside. A few were so badly crippled that they could no longer carry a load, but none died. In addition, that afternoon it first snowed and then rained. In all on this gloomy day (3 September) they managed to cover only eleven miles. It was very cold that night – how cold they could not tell, for the thermometer had been broken when one of the horses had slipped – and no game had been sighted, so they did not have very much to eat.

With some feeling, they called the gap in the mountains through which they had managed to find a passage, 'Lost Trail Pass'. In fact they were now over the worst, though they did not know it. All they could do was press on. Certainly things improved the next day, when they met for the first time a party of Flathead Indians who proved very friendly. Their name was derived from their peculiar appearance. When a baby of this tribe was born it was placed in a sort of trough and a pillow of wool or feathers was placed across its forehead. On top of this was placed a piece of wood so fitted that it would press down hard on the head. For a year the baby was left in this instrument of torture before being taken out with its forehead suitably flattened and broadened. The explorers were to discover that other Indian tribes also flattened their heads in a way they thought beautiful. Apparently, this pressure on the skull did not affect the Indians mentally. Only full members of the tribe had to submit to this flattening; their slaves did not undergo the treatment.

The expedition stayed two days at the Flatheads' village. All the party were tired and they needed more horses, as some of those they had started out with were almost worn out. By suitable bartering, Clark was able to exchange seven old horses and a quantity of trade goods for eleven new ones. They had no means of talking directly with the Indians and Toby could not give any assistance, but they listened with fascination to the deep gurgling speech of this people, which was quite different from any sound they had heard an Indian make before.

One of their abiding delusions was that somewhere along the way they would come across the 'Welsh Indians' about whom they had been told before they started. Three members of the expedition recorded in their diaries that they might at last have found this mythical tribe, who were supposed to be the descendants of the party from Wales that, according to tradition, sailed across the Atlantic with Prince Madoc in the

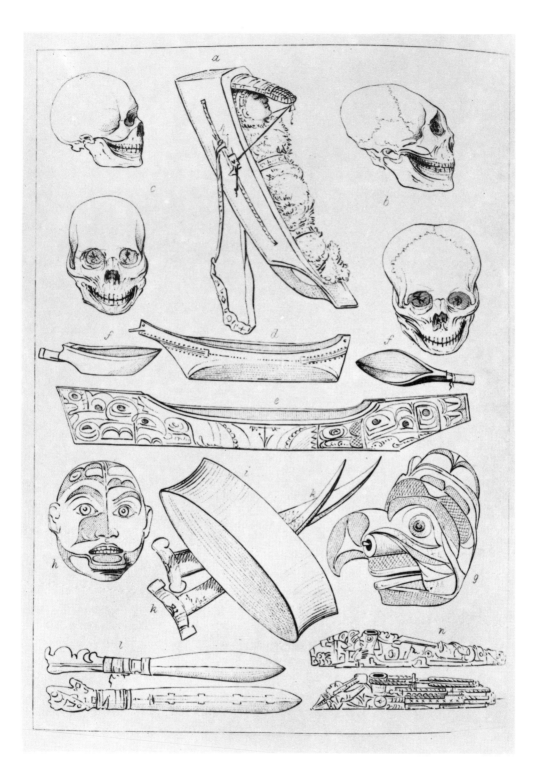

Drawings from George Catlin's notebook recording the custom from which the Flathead Indians derived their name.
ABOVE Flathead mother (a Chinook from the Columbia river valley) with her baby fitted into a wooden device designed to flatten and broaden the forehead
LEFT Papoose back-cradle with the flattening device and its effect on the skull (right) in contrast to the normal shape (left). Below are various knives, masks and other utensils of the tribe.

twelfth century. Certainly these men were paler than the Indians they had met previously, but no one could really mistake them for white men. Just in case these people should prove to be the missing Welsh tribe Lewis carefully wrote down phonetically a short vocabulary of their language, so that when they got back to civilisation they could compare the words with Welsh. It is not recorded that he ever did this, but later scholars have been able to find no similarity between the two languages.

They called this stopping-point Traveller's Rest. After their two-day break, much refreshed, they started off along a wooded valley with a fast-running creek at its bottom. There was even more game here and the hunters were able to kill four deer, a beaver and three grouse. The next day (10 September) John Coulter brought in three Flatheads he had found hunting for some stolen horses. They were questioned by sign language and told Lewis and Clark that they were now only 'five sleeps' from where they would be able to launch canoes on the Columbia river. This proved to be a very optimistic forecast, since it was more than ten days before they were through the worst of the mountains, but it cheered them up. They were not even abashed when Toby showed them a pass going eastwards which, he told them, would take them to the Great Falls of the Missouri in only five days. It had taken them fifty-one days to cover the same distance; but they would not have found the trail without a guide, nor, if they had come by the shorter route, would they have made contact with the Shoshone and obtained the horses they needed. All the same, it must have been a galling moment.

Now they had to face the next mountain crossing. There were no river valleys to help them this time, and they had to zigzag their way up steep mountainsides covered with sharp boulders and thickly wooded with pine trees. Fallen trees often lay across the path, and several times in making detours they lost the best track and had to cast about to find it again. Several of the horses fell and the party straggled out over the trail. It was not until ten o'clock that night that the last arrivals staggered in exhausted. To make things worse there was no game here, and they had to be content with soup made of the single pheasant that had been killed. Even the presence of hot springs did not excite them very much.

The next day they descended into a valley and headed wearily up an even stiffer climb, their progress hampered by heavy rain and occasional hail. Their food stocks were now exhausted, so they killed a colt from their stock of horses. At least they ate well that night beside a small stream which they named 'Colt Killed Creek' in commemoration of their dinner.

They now reached the river that they had been hoping to find, the Kooskooskee, or Clearwater. It was eighty yards wide at this point but far too fast-flowing for them to think of trying to launch canoes, even if they had been able to find trees large enough to construct any. Toby told them that it was no use trying to follow the bank of the river and that they must cross another mountain. The going was pretty tough here with loose stones that often upset the horses. One fell right down the hillside into the river; the explorers assumed that it must have been killed, but when a couple of the men clambered down to recover the baggage they discovered that the horse was not badly hurt, and after ten minutes they were able to lead it up to rejoin the party. As night fell they were still on the mountainside with snow banks all round them, but they found a flattish piece of ground where they could make a fire to cook the rest of the colt left over from the day before. They had to melt snow to obtain water. It was an uncomfortable night, as there was barely room on the flat for the whole party to stretch out.

In the morning Lewis and Clark held a conference and agreed that they would have to do something radical about getting more food. There seemed to be no game in these parts and the large straggling party was not a good hunting unit. So they decided that Clark should press on with six men on good horses to hunt and leave supplies ready for the main party. They would follow the waters of the Kooskooskee to where it joined the Snake river, where Toby told them they should find a large Nez Percé encampment. So Clark set off, following the trail with great difficulty, for the snow was now lying thick on the ground. The only way of finding the right route to follow was to look for the broken branches of trees, showing where loaded Indian horses had pushed their way through. The next day he was able to kill a stray horse, most of which he hung on a tree for the main party to find when it followed up. Then he came out of the mountains on to rolling plains. On 20 September he saw three boys in the distance and persuaded them to guide him to their village. There, after a few moments of suspicion, he was hospitably received. He and his party were fed on dried salmon and flour made from the camass root, a small sweet-tasting, onion-like plant of the lily family. The expedition were to eat a lot of it in the next few months.

It was fortunate that these Nez Percés were friendly, for the next day first Clark and then his companions became very sick. Clark at first thought that the trouble was that they had eaten too much, but it became clear that it was some kind of dysentery for the main party, after it had straggled in a couple of days later, was struck down too. When he was somewhat recovered Clark was kept busy dosing the rest of the party with Rush's pills, Glauber's salts and other purgatives. It was over a week before they were all fit enough to travel.

In the meantime, Clark had made contact with an important chief of the neighbourhood, Twisted Hair, one of the Indians whom the explorers found most helpful. He belonged to the same branch of the Nez Percé people who would, seventy years later, produce one of the most remarkable of all Indian leaders, Chief Joseph, who, goaded by the constant erosion of his territory and rights by the encroaching white man, took up arms and fought a brilliantly conceived campaign against the US Cavalry. He very nearly succeeded in leading his people to sanctuary in Canada.

Twisted Hair told Clark that his people were accustomed to going down the Columbia river in canoes, and that a few miles farther down the Kooskooskee they would find pine trees big enough to hollow out for boats. Gass, the chief carpenter, and those fit enough to travel were sent on in the last week of September to set up a camp, which they called Canoe Camp. By 4 October they had constructed five boats, four large ones and a smaller one for scouting ahead, by burning out the centre of the pine trees.

The problem now was what to do with the thirty-eight horses that they had brought with them and would need later for the journey back through the mountains. They rounded them up and branded them with a neat oblong bearing the legend 'US Capt. M. Lewis', then handed them over to Twisted Hair, who agreed to look after them until the expedition returned in the spring of the following year. They built a cache for all the saddles and some of the ammunition. Then they launched their canoes, and soon they were bowling down the Kooskooskee and into the Snake river which would take them into the Columbia proper.

6 'Great Joy... the Ocean'

LOUISIANA.

THIS WAS THE FIRST TIME on their whole long trip that they would be going with the stream. After a few days there was some delay when Gass's boat was holed and sank, but the water was only waist-deep at the time and they managed to save all the supplies. This was only the first of a number of upsets; others were more serious. When Drewyer's boat overturned they lost a parcel of trade goods; this was a blow, for they were getting short, and these supplies represented their ready cash for trading with the Indians. As they passed from the Snake towards the main stream they were making their way through fairly well populated parts. Their way was eased partly by the presence of Twisted Hair and one of his sons, whom they had taken along as guides; but the Nez Percé chief told Lewis and Clark that it was really the sight of Sacajawea in their canoes that ensured them a friendly welcome. His people could not believe that a party which had hostile intent would bring a woman along with them.

All the people who lived in these parts existed on a diet of fish, mostly salmon, and roots. The salmon season was ending and there was little fresh fish to be had. The Indians were happy enough to eat the salmon they had dried on scaffolds that they constructed by the river, but the members of the expedition rapidly grew tired of this diet and, perhaps rightly, blamed their stomach troubles on the dried fish. There was no game in the region, and the French boatmen took to buying dogs from the local Indians and eating them. At first Lewis and Clark and the other Kentuckians were reluctant to join them, but the smell of roasting flesh was too much for them, and soon the expedition was buying dogs whenever it could. There were usually some to spare from the large number that roamed round the Indian villages. The Indians in this area never touched dog flesh, and referred to the explorers contemptuously as 'The Dog Eaters'.

As they came out on 16 October from the Snake into the great river, half a mile wide, it might have been thought that since they were now on the last leg of their outward journey the explorers would have mentioned in their diaries how they were at last floating down the Columbia. They made no special comment, however; probably because ahead of them, instead of a country of wide plains sloping gently down to the ocean, they saw the snow-capped peaks of the Cascade Mountains. Clark, scouting ahead, saw two outstanding

PREVIOUS PAGE Map of the Lewis and Clark expedition published in Peter Gass's *Journal of Voyages* in 1812.

142

mountains which turned out to be Mount Adams and Mount Hood. There was another range to pass through before their journey's end.

Still, things were going well. The various families of the Nez Percé nation, each with their distinctive clothing though all speaking the same language, came to call. One chief came with a procession of two hundred followers and a band of drums, but sometimes no word of the explorers' presence went ahead of them, so that their arrival caused consternation. On one occasion Clark was scouting ahead with Drewyer and the Fields brothers. He saw a crane flying overhead and shot it. Then, seeing a village of five matting huts, he made towards it. From the distance he could see people moving about, but when he came close, shooting a duck on the way, he found no sign of life. Eventually one of the frightened Indians emerged. By sign language Clark discovered that the Indians had seen the birds falling from the sky, and they had assumed that Clark must have descended from the air as well. The gift of a piece of

Young braves from the Nez Percé, Lewis and Clark's favourite nation. from Catlin's journal.

ribbon persuaded the Indians that the four white men meant
no harm and they were soon firm friends. They were passing
through rather barren country, sometimes between almost
desert plains with only rough grass growing in the sands; then
the rocky hills would close in on either side of the river. Every
so often there would be rapids, with rocks sticking up from the
water. The canoes were often in danger of upset, but thanks to
their Indian guides there were no disasters.

On one island they saw a large structure made out of
assorted pieces of wood. It was sixty feet long and twelve feet
wide, constructed round a frame of pine logs, the walls being
made of pieces of plank and an old canoe. When they went
inside they found that it was the local burial house. Clark
recorded with some surprise:

... in it I observed great numbers of humane bones of every descrip-
tion perticularly in a pile near the center of the vault, in the East end
21 Scul bones forming a circle on the mats; the westerly part of the
Vault appeared to be appropriated for those of more resent death,
as many of the bodies of the deceased raped up in leather robes, lay in
row on boards covered with mats etc.

Round the bodies were large collections of goods that the dead
warriors might need on their journey to the next world. It
also looked as if horses had been sacrificed to provide for their
future transport.

All the Indians they had talked to had warned them that
they soon would be coming to rapids and waterfalls, now known
as the Celilo Falls. In fact they arrived above them on 22
October. They were not as wonderful a sight as the Missouri
falls, but it would take a brave man to try and shoot them in a
canoe. And the brave man was there – William Clark. The big
canoes were not at all easy to carry over the rocky shores, and
here there was no overland route along which they could wheel
a boat. They unloaded the canoes, and carried the goods and
manhandled the boats as well as they could for a little way.
Then Clark determined to try shooting the rapids. Cruzatte,
the best of the boatmen, agreed to go with him, and they made
the passage successfully.

The Nez Percé guides now proved very reluctant to go any
farther. They did not, they said, speak the language of the
people below the falls, who were quite likely to attack the party.
Even if the white men were not killed, they, as traditional

At the Celilo Falls, showing members of the expedition 'portaging' a canoe – from a mural in the Rotunda at Salem, Oregon.

enemies, certainly would not escape. It took all Lewis's power of persuasion to make them continue, but finally they agreed. As they made the portage of the goods, all the party checked their arms in case of attack, but none came. In fact, the Indians – a branch of the Chinook nation – who lived below the falls proved to be as friendly as the Nez Percé. They lent horses to help carry the heavy goods, showed the explorers their fish traps, and displayed their skill in handling their light canoes. So impressed was Lewis with the seaworthiness of these vessels that he traded the smallest of his dugouts for one of these Chinook craft. These Indians made the expedition another present that they were less happy to receive. They dried their

fish on straw which was infested with fleas, and from then on
through the winter the explorers were plagued by the bites of
these insects. Lewis tried to do a bit of peacemaking while he
was there, and his Nez Percé guides agreed to make peace with
their neighbours below the falls.

When the holes made in the canoes in shooting the rapids
had been patched, the expedition set out again. They encountered a whole series of rapids as they threaded their way
through the Cascade Mountains. Sometimes they managed to
shoot the rock-strewn water, and sometimes they were able to
steer the empty boats through the rough parts from the shore
by means of elk-skin ropes. Once there was no other way but to

take the canoes ashore and roll them along on a series of logs.

When they were coming to the end of the rapids, they noticed something that made their hearts leap; observing the river, they could see that at last they were in tidal waters. The ocean could not be very far now. And there were other signs. An Indian in a canoe who called at their camp one night was dressed in what was unmistakably a British sailor's jacket. Some of the Indians, too, knew a word or two of English they had learned from the crews of trading ships which came every now and then to the mouth of the Columbia river. One important Chinook chief whom they met on 29 October had a fine coat of scarlet and blue cloth and a sword given him by European visitors who had come from the sea. For all the sophistication of his ceremonial clothing, the explorers were taken aback when this same chief told his wife to produce his medicine bag. This proved to be decorated with fourteen forefingers which he had hung there as trophies of enemies killed in battle. These, Clark noted, were the first Indians he had come across who did not take scalps.

Just as the explorers' spirits were being raised by their obvious closeness to their goal – sea otters were now swimming round the canoes – the weather changed. The days alternated between rain and fog. Sometimes one of the boats would get detached from the party and they would have to wait until the weather cleared before they could be reunited. On the evening of 3 November Whitehouse recorded in his diary: 'Towards evening we met Several Indians in a canoe who were going up the River, they signed to us that in two Sleeps we Should See the Ocean, vessels and White people etc, etc.' This showed them how wrong information gained by sign language could sometimes be. It was not until four days later that Clark was writing: 'Great joy in the camp . . . we are in view of the Ocean. In the morning when the fog cleared off just below the last village this great Pacific Ocean which we had been so long anxious to see and the roreing or noise made by the waves brakeing in on the rocky shores may be heard distictly.' Joy indeed, but in fact they had not arrived at the open sea, and there were no ships and white men there to greet them. They had been driven by the winds and the high waves into one of the bays (Grays Bay) on the north side of the Columbia river estuary.

Though they had arrived at their journey's end, or appeared

OPPOSITE ABOVE Camp just before the Rockies, from a mid nineteenth-century watercolour.
BELOW 'Study of a Grizzly' by W.R. Leigh. The grizzly bear has been the subject of numerous legends of the West and has been ruthlessly persecuted, almost to extinction. Lewis and Clark record many hair-raising encounters with grizzlies, but, although dangerous and difficult to kill, these animals are almost wholly vegetarians.

amic ou castor

Loup marin

3 tygre marin

Page from a sketch book of Charles Bécard de Granville, a seventeenth-century French Canadian, showing a sea-otter, a beaver and sea-lions.

to have, there could be no relaxing. The coast on which they had been driven ashore was very inhospitable. Sheer rocks rose directly from the tideline, so that they could not lay out their soaking clothes and goods to dry and there was no level surface where they could make camp. The hunters managed to scramble up the rocks and were able to kill some ducks and geese which gave them some welcome fresh meat. The whole party then set off again to look for a more hospitable harbour. They were so tossed about in their lightweight canoes that several of the party were seasick. The new cove that they found was hardly more comfortable, though they were able to construct a log platform on which to place their goods in the hope of drying them, and to lie above the tideline to sleep. A scouting party was sent out in the Indian canoe to prospect the coast but it was soon forced back by high winds and huge waves.

In a calmer spell the whole party took to the water again and found yet another cove a little closer to the Pacific. They needed water now, for what the estuary supplied was far too salty for them to drink, and though it was raining most of the time the water they could collect was not much of a ration for thirty-two thirsty souls. Fields took his gun on a hunting trip, but found that the undergrowth on the rocky land above the camp was so thick that he could not cut his way through, so he came back empty-handed.

The only thing to do was try even nearer to the river mouth. A reconnaissance party had found a small Indian encampment, and the party made its way there. The hinterland was slightly more passable here, so Lewis with three men set off to scout down the coast by land. They hoped they might find the white traders the Indians had told them about, but they were unsuccessful and had to turn back. Clark then took a larger party (York and ten others) and set off for a full-scale investigation of the whole of the north coast of the Columbia estuary as far as Cape Disappointment. Although they had managed to kill some game, it was obvious that there was not enough in this rugged land to keep them supplied throughout the long winter they must spend here. The Indians on this coast were not very friendly. Two hunters had had their guns stolen from under their pillows while they slept, and Lewis had had to visit the Indian camp with an armed party who, by threatening gestures, managed to recover the weapons. Any more stealing, he said, and he would shoot the culprits.

Clark, however, met two important chiefs, the one-eyed Comcommoly and Chillahlawil who, after he had given them medals, seemed to be prepared to be hospitable. (The former ruled over his people long enough to welcome, nearly a decade later, the party that arrived to set up Astoria, the great centre for the beaver trade that was to be built near this point and was to provide the basis for the fortune of the Astor family.) Clark saw one of the Indians wearing a magnificent sea-otter skin robe and tried to bargain for it. The only thing that the owner would accept for it was blue beads, and the only ones they had were a string that Sacajawea was wearing round her waist.

It may seem hard that she had to give up her finery, but she did it as usual without complaint. Clark recorded laconically: 'We procured it for a belt of blue beeds which the squar-wife of our interpreter Shabono wore around her waste.'

One thing that Clark's expedition had made clear was that they would have to look elsewhere for their winter quarters. A canoe-load of Clatsop Indians, a sub-family of the Chinooks, who had come across to see Lewis, told him that there was more game on the south side of the river mouth. It was now really urgent that they should find winter quarters. The continual rain and spray brought in by the gales was rotting their clothes and their moccasins. The buffalo robes they slept in were always soaking, and all the Indians seemed to be able to offer them for food was dried fish and flour made from the dried and powdered arrowhead root which they did not find particularly palatable. Taking advantage of a break in the weather, Lewis took a party across by canoe to prospect the southern shore. He found a site on a rising bit of ground a few miles up a creek now called the Lewis and Clark river. The site seemed fairly dry, compared with the universally boggy land in the surrounding area, so he came back to fetch the rest of the party. Before they left they all carved their names on trees as the sign of the terminal point of the outward journey; then they thankfully left that miserable northern shore.

Had they stayed there a few more days, they would have seen a ship putting in. For some reason the Indians did not tell the ship's crew that there were white men across the river mouth nor, though they visited the explorers frequently during the winter, did they tell Lewis and Clark that the ship had called. Perhaps this was just caution, or perhaps there was a more sinister motive. They may have thought that the party, which must have looked pretty bedraggled by now, would not last through the winter and there would be riches to be picked up later on. Because of this, Lewis lost the chance of sending back a message to Washington announcing their arrival. This ship was not sent by Jefferson; he seems to have forgotten to arrange for one, or if he did no record remains of it. The way home would have to be once again the long trek by land.

Captain Clark & h

building a line of Huts

ON 10 DECEMBER THEY STARTED WORK on constructing a square fort out of pine logs. It would consist of seven huts and in the centre there would be a sort of yard twenty feet across. At least it would be dry. Clark, the great woodsman who loathed the sea, could now relax. Only one week earlier – presumably he was feeling under the weather, for he developed an attack of dysentery the next day – he had noted in his diary:

The emence Seas and waves . . . and this roaring has continued since our arrival in the neighbourhood of the Sea Coast which has been 24 days Since we arrived in Sight of the Great Western (for I cannot say Pacific) Ocian as I have not seen one pacific day Since my arrival in the vicinity, and its waters are foaming and perpetually breake with the emence waves on the Sands and rockey coasts, tempestuous and horiable.

'Tempestuous and horiable' are the best words to describe the winter that followed. Only on twelve days did it not rain, and of these only six were sunny. Although it was set back from the coast, Fort Clatsop was still in the path of the gales that blew in from the ocean almost without cease. At least there was plenty of elk meat, though unfortunately they were totally out of salt which they needed not only for flavouring but for preserving the meat. In the very damp atmosphere the meat soon went off and they found that they were wasting a great deal. All their efforts went into completing the fort, and finally on 30 December the flag was raised as a sign of the completion of the work. The local Indians had been in the habit of wandering in and out at any time, but now Lewis gave instructions that the gate of the fort was to be shut between sundown and dawn.

It was a dull and dreary time for everyone except the two leaders, who spent the next few months writing up their notes of the outward voyage, completing their maps and recording the wild life and natural features they had observed on the way. For the men the most constant diversion was a sort of brothel near the camp presided over by an old squaw who had 'six nieces', all readily available. Two of the men caught venereal infections, but these were kept under control by the French Canadians who had their own remedies. The wet weather also took its toll. Nearly all the party suffered from rheumatic pains from sleeping perpetually in wet bedclothes, and they often had colds. Only Bratton was seriously ill. His back pains – modern doctors, examining the evidence in the

OPPOSITE ABOVE Camp at the source of the Columbia river.

BELOW Charles Russell's watercolour, 'The Robe Traders' is based on the western fur trade of the early nineteenth century. The leading Indian of the Blackfoot tribe signals his readiness for bargaining to the white men in the trading post.

Fort Clatsop which has been faithfully reconstructed from Captain Clark's floor plan dimensions. Strict military routine was preserved at the fort. A sentinel was posted at all times and the gates were shut against all outsiders from dusk to dawn.

leaders' diaries, are uncertain whether these arose from an ailment in the lower back or from a stomach infection – were crippling and he was not able to do much work for months.

There were only two regular occupations, hunting and salt making. Two hunting parties were always out, shooting for the pot and also securing the hides that the men would need for their clothing on the return journey. As for salt making, the only way they could secure enough of this vital condiment was to station six men at a camp on the edge of the ocean. Here they kept six kettles of sea water perpetually boiling in order to extract the salt. They found that by this method they could collect four quarts of salt a day. Perhaps because they had been without salt so long, the leaders pronounced this product to be as good as the rock salt they had found in the United States. Only on one day did they do no work at all and that was Christmas Day. This occasion was described rather sadly by Clark:

At day light this morning we were awoke by the discharge of the fire arms of all our party & a Selute, Shouts and a Song which the whole party joined in under our windows, after wich they retired to their rooms [and] were chearful all the morning. after brackfast we divided our tobacco which amounted to 12 carrots [quarts] one half of which we gave to the men of the party who used tobacco, and to those who doe not use it we make a present of a handkerchief. The Indians leave us in the evening. all the party snugly fixed in their huts. I receivd a present from Capt L. of a fleece shirt, Drawers and socks, a par of Mockersons of Whitehouse, a small Indian basket of Gutherich, two Dozen white weazil tails of the Indian woman [Sacajawea] & some black root [it was like liquorice] of the Indians before their departure. . . . We would have Spent this day of the nativity of Christ in feasting, had we any thing either to raise our Sperits or even gratify our appetites, our Diner consisting of pore Elk, so much Spoiled that we eate it thro' mear necessity, Some Spoiled pounded fish and a few roots.

A fortnight later, Sacajawea ceased for once to be the submissive wife, when she heard that a whale had been stranded on the shore quite near where the salt boilers were encamped. Having come all this way with the party, she insisted that she must go and see 'the big fish'. She got her way, but the sight must have been something of a disappointment. By the time she arrived, the local Indians had cut off all the blubber and only the bones and some rotting flesh remained. Still, the expedition was given a share of the fat, which was helpful since they were almost out of candles and the whale tallow supplied new ones.

As February went on its way, they began to think about starting for home. The Indians of the mountains had told them that it was no use their starting much before April, because the snow made the trails through the mountains impassable. Though they were not well stocked with food – the hunters found that the elk were getting lean and did not provide nearly as much meat at the end of the winter – they could probably get by until they reached the areas which were better supplied, but they were desperately short of trade goods. All that they had left was six 'carrots' of tobacco (half of the total stock that they had divided on Christmas Day) and a few other trade goods that could be wrapped up in two handkerchiefs. They had been far too lavish on the early part of the trip, having hoped to contact a ship and exchange one of their letters of credit for trade goods. Now they tried offering money, but the Chinooks were not at all interested. They did not even want axes or knives; they wanted trinkets. Lewis and Clark managed to stay on friendly terms with the local grand chief, a man that they got on with very well, by giving him a pair of

Lewis and Clark on the Columbia
river. Sacajawea. papoose
on her back, and her husband
Charbonneau, the French
trader, stand behind them.

silk pantaloons, but blue beads and the like were in woefully short supply. There were a few unpleasant 'incidents. Once Whitehouse, paying a call on one of the local lodges, had to run for his life when he found that he was being lured into a dark corner by a squaw so that her husband could knife him for what he possessed – a blanket and a few odds and ends. Lewis immediately turned out the guard and the Indian apologised.

For the rest of the time they had to sit and wait. They had plenty of Indians for company, but these Chinooks were by no means their favourites; they were shifty and rather grimy. The men wore long tunics, but the women only wore short ones reaching to the waist, with a kind of petticoat below, made of a material woven from bark. This under-garment was, Lewis recorded, long enough to keep the woman decent when she was erect, 'but when she stoops or places herself in many other attitudes, this battery of Venus is not altogether impervious to the iniquisitive and penetrating eye of the amorite'. The Indians spent much of their time gambling. The principal game seemed to be a simplified form of 'Find the Lady'. The banker held a piece of bone which he passed from hand to hand while his audience made bets as to which hand it would finally be in when he held them up for choice.

The time must have passed very slowly waiting for 1 April, the nominated starting day. In the event the commanders decided not to wait so long. They had to choose between two evils. If they waited until April, there was a chance that a trading ship might come up the coast, so that they could replenish their supplies; but if they dallied too long they might not get home that year at all. They needed more light canoes for the upriver journey, but their bargaining power was very small. Eventually they got one first-class canoe in exchange for Lewis's laced coat of a captain in the infantry. He recorded sadly that the army owed him a coat, but he felt that the sacrifice was worth while. Another canoe was confiscated as a reprisal against some Indians for stealing meat. The only thing the party was really well stocked with was hides for clothing, and of these they had more than ever before; there was enough leather for about three hundred pairs of moccasins. They were as ready as they were ever going to be, so there was no point in staying.

On 22 March they abandoned Fort Clatsop, their final

Scientific Instruments of the Expedition

Explorers in the early nineteenth century had none of the advantages of modern scientific equipment. Lewis and Clark set out to explore a totally unchartered territory and with the use of only a few instruments to help them.

RIGHT A 50-foot linen measuring tape with a book-form leather carrying case which also holds a note pad and pencil, as used by surveyors in the 1800s.

LEFT A pocket sextant made in the late 1700s. Using a compass, a sextant and a watch, explorers were able to make rough maps, chart rivers and fix their position.

LEFT A 'universal instrument' of the 1800s used to measure the horizon angle between two distant objects, or angles of elevation or depression. The simple graduated scale provided the tangent of the angle.

BELOW Lewis's compass, now in the Smithsonian Institute.

gesture being to give Camowool, the local chief, a certificate of good conduct. They paddled off across to the northern shore of the estuary, intending to follow the same route upriver as they had used on the journey down, but the sea was too rough for them to make any headway that day. The next morning, however, they set off again. By 1 April they were proceeding steadily up the Columbia river, begging and buying what food they could from the encampments they passed. Their diet was now composed of dried fish and powdered wapatoo root with an occasional dog thrown in. Several canoe-loads of Indians who had come down from the Columbia rapids told them that the food situation was bad; the new season's salmon would not be arriving until May, and everyone there was hungry. Lewis immediately sent out hunting-parties to shoot what they could, but they were not able to find much game, only enough to keep them going, with a little left over which they dried for future use.

The Indians must have sensed that Lewis and Clark were now short of trade goods, for they became increasingly surly. One group refused absolutely to accept any of the goods that Clark offered in return for wapatoo root. In a moment of inspiration he decided to try a bit of magic on them. Feeling in his pocket for a port-fire match he threw it into the Indians' fire, where it burnt with a lurid sulphur flame. At the same time he produced his pocket compass and, with a magnet which he happened to have in his inkhorn, made the compass rotate rapidly. The Indians were so frightened by these demonstrations that they begged Clark to take what he wanted and 'put out the bad fire'. When the match burned itself out, Clark paid for what he took at his own price, calmly smoked a pipe with the Indians and left.

So they made their way to the first rapids in the Cascade Mountains. Going up these was going to be difficult. The rapids were running faster than when they had shot them coming down; they had to empty the canoes, carry all the goods to the top of each section of rapids and then go back to the hard struggle of towing the canoes up. The party was not as fit as it might have been – Bratton was still in agony from his bad back and three of the others were limping through rheumatism. The weather was still wet most of the time, so the invalids had not much chance to recover. The local Indians were not at all helpful; they just stood around, pinching the

odd axe or piece of iron when they could. Sometimes there were
more serious incidents. On one occasion, when Shields had
bought a dog for food, two Indians snatched it away from him.
He immediately drew his only weapon, a long hunting knife,
and rushed towards them before they could fit arrows to their
bows. Seeing his determination they dropped the dog and ran
away.

But all the time there were jeering crowds of Indians milling
around. Lewis felt that it was necessary to take strong action:
he told them that if there was any more trouble he would shoot
the thief out of hand. This brought the local chief down to the
scene. He told Lewis that his people were being incited by two
bad characters from another tribe, and promised that they
would now behave. As a result he was given a small medal and
the situation calmed down. Things were so much improved
that one of the small canoes which had been taken ahead by
the hunters and which had broken away from its moorings
was returned by the Indians. For this the finders were rewarded
with an axe and a piece of iron. But if the expedition gained

Meeting with an Indian; by
Frederic Remington.

a canoe that day, the next they lost one when, in dragging one of the bigger boats through rough water, the tow-ropes broke and the craft was dashed to pieces as it was carried down the rapids.

This loss caused a change of plan. They tried redistributing the load among the remaining two large and five small canoes, but when they were overloaded like this they were almost impossible to handle. Clearly river travel was going to become increasingly difficult. Not only had they to complete the passage of the Cascade rapids but they had also to tackle the Celilo Falls. It would be quicker going by land if they could find the necessary horses to carry the baggage. Clark went on ahead to see if he could buy any. He was by now becoming an expert at barter with very small resources, exchanging their elk skins for the blue beads which were the acceptable substitute for cash in most transactions. At the next village he found a further expedient which was to keep them going over the next few weeks. When he tried to buy horses, he was refused or asked utterly exorbitant prices. Then he noticed that the local chief was suffering from unpleasant sores on his body, and produced some ointment to cure them. The chief was immensely pleased and proceeded to parade his wife for consultation as well. Clark describes what happened: 'his wife who I found to be a sulky Bitch was somewhat efflicted with pains in her back. I rubed a little camphere on her temples and back, and applyed worm flannel to her back which she thought had nearly restored her to her former feelings. this I thought a favourable time to trade . . . I according made the Chief an offer which he excepted and sold me two horses.'

Many of the Indians in this area suffered from some sort of eye ailment. Lewis and Clark mixed up some palliative drops which they found were very good bargaining counters. But for all his efforts Clark only managed to acquire four horses, so the leaders decided on a compromise: the light canoes would continue as far as possible and the larger ones would be chopped up for firewood. But after a short while river travel became too difficult even for a small canoe if it carried any baggage. Two were kept for use in hunting and two more were bartered for goods which they could later exchange for horses. The remaining one was in such a bad condition that they chopped it up.

Again there was trouble with Indians stealing. In the hope of getting better trading terms Lewis overlooked some minor thefts, but the matter seemed to be getting out of hand. One man who was caught in the act of stealing an axe was roughly thrown out of their encampment, and Lewis threatened to burn the Indian village down if there was any more trouble. After this he managed to get two more horses, but lost another that had not been properly tied up. This horse had been caught by an Indian, but he then lost it in gambling with a man from another tribe who made off with it. After much effort it was finally recovered. In all they managed to buy or hire ten horses. Led by an Indian guide, they made their way by land towards Twisted Hair's village. The going was not at all easy; though the land was flat enough, it was alternately rocky and sandy. The Indians were now quite aware of the explorers' poverty and drove hard bargains for every dog needed for food. When the travellers finally decided to dispose of the last canoes, the Choppunish people (a branch of the Nez Percé) they were staying with at the time refused to trade anything for them. Lewis ordered his men to chop them up, but after the first axe blow

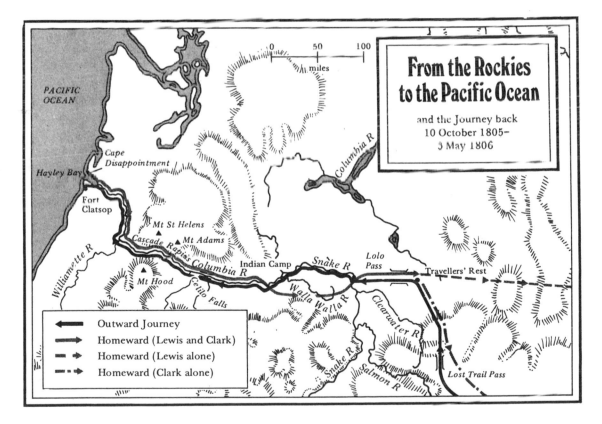

Interior of an Indian hut,
the hole in the roof forming
the chimney.

the Indians agreed to give a string of blue beads for each one.

The situation improved slightly a couple of days later when they arrived at the villages ruled by Yellept, the chief of the Wallawalla people, who lived near the point where the Snake river flowed into the Columbia. This group of the Nez Percé Lewis called 'the most honest hospitable and sincere' of any tribe they met. It was a great change to have Yellept himself bringing them a present of firewood and fresh fish and offering Clark a good grey horse for his own use. The chief wanted a kettle in return, but was not put out when it was explained that they did not have one to spare and said that he would accept anything that Clark liked to give him. Touched by this rare generosity, Clark handed over his sword and a quantity of powder and shot.

In the event Yellept was almost too hospitable; he did not want to let his guests leave, insisting that they must stay and dance with him. They did so for a couple of days and then borrowed two canoes from him to ferry their equipment across the river so that they could make their way between the Columbia and Snake rivers direct to the Clearwater. A day after the party had set off, Lewis was astonished to see one of Yellept's men riding hard to catch them up. In his hand was a steel trap which had been left behind by accident. This action was regarded by the explorers as an unparalleled piece of honesty.

The next part of the journey was pleasant enough; the land they were crossing was fairly easy going. The snow-capped Bitter Root Mountains were in sight, and another week would bring them to Twisted Hair's camp. The Indians of these parts – they met many along the way – had heard of Clark's prowess as a 'doctor' and came to him with their eye troubles and rheumatic pains. In fact the phials of eye water, which he and Lewis carefully ensured contained no harmful matter, kept the travellers provisioned; the Indians were happy to pay in dogs, fish and roots for the attention they received. There was only one unpleasant incident, when the party was sitting down eating one night: a boy cheekily threw a half-starved dog at Lewis, saying something offensive about dog-eaters. The commander would not put up with behaviour like this; he leapt up, hurled the dog back in the boy's face and threatened him with a tomahawk.

On 5 May they finally arrived in Twisted Hair's country,

wondering whether they would find the thirty-eight horses that they had left there the autumn before. Without them they would have a difficult job crossing the mountains, and they certainly had not enough goods to trade for a new baggage train. The first chief they met, Cut Nose – so called because his face had been slashed in battle, giving him a rather horrible expression – was evasive, so the expedition took him with them to meet Twisted Hair. Their old friend did not seem at all pleased to see them. Lewis and Clark realised that something was going on between the two chiefs, but a Shoshone prisoner of Cut Nose who could speak the Choppunish language refused to translate what was being said. Eventually a superior chief, Broken Arm, arrived and took part in the argument. It turned out that Cut Nose and Broken Arm had been away when the expedition had passed through on its way west. According to Twisted Hair, they were jealous of the fact that he had been given charge of the horses. They had insisted on sharing the job, and the subsequent reward. After much argument he had agreed to this. The horses had been divided, but they had also been allowed to wander all over the place. Cut Nose's version was different: he said that Twisted Hair had been letting his warriors ride the horses too hard and that he (Cut Nose) had only intervened to save the horses. After several days spent in rounding up the animals, all except two were recovered. These had apparently been taken by Toby, their Shoshone guide, who had run away from the expedition the year before without being paid.

A solemn council was held to try to reconcile the quarrelling chiefs. Lewis made one of his most eloquent speeches which was translated first into French, then by Charbonneau into Minnetaree, then by Sacajawea into Shoshone and finally, by the prisoner who had been reluctant to translate earlier, into Choppunish. It was a somewhat longwinded process – the council lasted all night – but it seemed to work well enough, though it was fairly obvious that the two chiefs would never stay friends.

After Cut Nose left, suitably rewarded with medals and a pistol, relations with Twisted Hair improved. He told them that it was no use their trying to make their way through the mountain passes until the next new moon (1 June). This rather disheartened the party, who wanted to be on their way. If they waited, Twisted Hair told them, he was prepared to let two of his sons go with them as guides. They had no alternative but to agree, and spent their time in 'medical' work, including 'sweating' a totally paralysed chief. This involved enclosing him in a sort of clay oven and lighting a fire underneath so as to make him sweat violently. Lewis and Clark first tried this treatment out on Bratton, who was still suffering considerable pain; it gave him some relief. Fortunately it also helped the old chief, who, having been unable to move a muscle for months, was able to wash his own face the day after the operation. There was very little food to be had, but in return for the medical attention the expedition slowly built up a stock of roots, some of which were pounded into flour and then baked into bread, ready for the journey through the mountains.

It turned out to be fortunate that the party was delayed in the lowlands, because several of them fell ill, possibly with some form of influenza, and it would have been difficult to nurse them in the mountain snows. The most dangerously ill was Sacajawea's sixteen-month-old baby, who developed a serious throat infection which lasted for more than a fortnight. Lewis and Clark treated this sickness as well as they could by giving the child doses of cream of tartar and putting onion poultices on his neck.

The whole party had slowly been making its way with its Indian companions towards the mountains, hoping that the half-dozen or so invalids would recover. On 1 June they had a sad blow when one of their baggage horses slipped and fell with its load from a cliff into the river below. An Indian swam out to recover as much of the load as he could, but most of it was carried away, including the last of their paint, a most useful item of barter. Later the same day a raft carrying their bread and root supplies across a river was overturned and the whole cargo was lost. They were now without food and had virtually no merchandise. Hastily they made a search for possible objects to be bartered. Among other things, they cut off all their remaining coat buttons and sent McNeill and York with these and some empty tin boxes and phials of eye water to the nearest village to try to buy some fresh food supplies. They were fortunate, returning with three bushels of roots and bread. This was a success, wrote Clark, 'not much less pleasing to us than the return of a good cargo to an East India merchant'.

Hunting-parties bought in some further small supplies of fish and meat, and on 8 June Lewis and Clark made up their

The formidable mountain range over which the expedition had to make its way twice.

minds to start the mountain crossing. The Indians still coun-
selled delay for another month, but the explorers refused to
listen to them; if they waited any longer they would not be
able to get to the Mandans before the Missouri froze for the
winter. On 16 June they had reached the bottom of Hungry
Creek where, on the way out, Clark had gone on ahead to meet
Twisted Hair for the first time. At this point they said goodbye
to the chief, presenting to him a gun and ammunition as a
reward for looking after the horses, and headed up into the
snows. But they had to go alone; Twisted Hair had changed
his mind about letting his sons go as guides.

8 Over the Top -   and Beyond

ABOVE Blue Spring, Lower Geyser Basin, Yellowstone by Thomas Moran. The steaming springs were much appreciated by the expedition, Lewis managing to bathe in the hot water for nineteen minutes.

PREVIOUS PAGES
The Snake river.

THEY MADE THEIR WAY up Hungry Creek and, as the track beside the stream petered out, up the mountainside. Here they found themselves rapidly coming into the deep snows. Lewis estimated that there was fifteen or sixteen feet of snow at this point. It seemed firm enough to bear the horses, but all the landmarks were blotted out and it was obvious that they could not make their way through this wilderness without guides. Lewis and Clark estimated that it would take about five days to reach Traveller's Rest; there was no chance of finding any grass for their horses in this period and there seemed to be no game around to feed the men. The leaders decided that the only thing to do was to erect a scaffold to hold their heavy equipment and make their way back to the villages to try to bribe someone to show them the way. Going down again was difficult, and they lost two of the horses before they reached the villages. In the next few days they had more luck with hunting, shooting several bears and some deer. Better still, Drewyer came across two Indians who were prepared to come with them over the mountains and who claimed to know the way.

On 24 June they were on their way again. To bring good luck for the journey the guides set fire to a copse of fir trees that grew by the trail. The burning needles made a fine firework display. Once more they threaded their way up Hungry Creek and on to the hillside above. Soon they were back at the point where they had left their baggage. With full loads they led their horses up over the deep snow, which was still firm enough to take them. When they crossed the ridge they found much less snow on the farther side, and there was even some grass showing so that the horses could crop. One of their guides complained of feeling sick, but they thought that this was only a customary piece of Indian duplicity because he did not want to go any farther. They were, however, suitably remorseful that night when they discovered that he was really ill, and gave him a buffalo robe to sleep under.

The next morning the guide was better. They made their way up a steep ridge, deep in snow, until they reached a cairn constructed by Indians out of pine-wood and stone which marked the highest point on the route. At the request of their guides they stopped and smoked a solemn pipe at this spot. To their surprise they were moving at an astonishingly good pace over the hard-packed snow, though they realised how wise

they had been in not trying to make the crossing by themselves. The blaze-marks on the trees were few and far between, and they could very easily have been lost. Up and down over the ridges they went, camping in the snow at night. There was no grass for the horses now and they were beginning to look gaunt. The hunters had only been able to shoot an occasional bird. Then quite suddenly on 29 June they were out of the snows and making their way down through the meadows to Traveller's Rest Creek. They reckoned that their journey through the mountains had measured one hundred and fifty-six miles.

It was time to rest and make plans for the future. After the cold of the mountains they were happy to give themselves baths in the hot springs that gushed out of the earth near the creek. As one always eager to make a scientific experiment, Lewis tried to see how long he could sit in the scalding spring. He managed nineteen minutes before he emerged bathed in sweat. As a relaxation the white men ran races against their Indian guides, who also gave exhibitions of horsemanship. In the evening they got down to the serious business of dividing the expedition into five different parties for the next stage of the journey. While they had been waiting at Fort Clatsop, Lewis and Clark had discussed endlessly the fact that they knew they had come a long way round. If they were to do a proper job of exploration it was essential that both the shorter alternative routes should be examined. It was decided that Lewis should call for six volunteers – they turned out to be Drewyer, the Fields brothers, Gass, Frazier and Werner – to go the short way over the mountain passes to the Great Falls of the Missouri. They would then explore Maria's river to see whether this was an easy route to Canada, then go on to meet the canoe party and proceed with them to the point where the Yellowstone joined the Missouri. With them would go three others, Thompson, Goodrich and McNeill, who would recover the pirogue left by the Great Falls and load it with the goods they had cached nearby, ready to join the canoe party as it came down from the Shoshone villages.

Meanwhile Clark would take the rest of expedition to the Shoshone villages to collect the goods and canoes left there. Then he, with ten men and Sacajawea, would cross the mountains to the Yellowstone, travelling by horse, and continue down it to a point where they could build canoes and

Indians hunting buffalo. The horses were specially trained for the work and were the hunters' most prized possessions.

launch them to make the rest of the journey to the Missouri by boat. Pryor and two men would take the horses by land to the rendezvous point. The remaining men, Ordway and nine others, would go by boat from the Shoshone villages, join up with Thompson at the Falls and then pick up Lewis and his party and proceed downriver. By 3 July all the firearms had been checked – Shields, the armourer, had been working solidly for two days – and the supplies divided. The parties went their separate ways. For the first time for more than two years they ceased to be part of a united team. Now even if all went well it would be six weeks before they met again.

It was perhaps a portent of trouble to come that just before he set out Lewis was thrown from his horse and fell forty feet down a steep hillside, followed by his mount. Happily neither of them was badly hurt. Slightly bruised, Lewis rode off, accompanied by the Indian guides who agreed to see him on his way over the pass (later to be called Lewis and Clark Pass, though in fact Clark never saw it). The going was surprisingly easy; the paths were not too steep and they could follow creek beds most of the way. Within a couple of days they were on a magnificent rolling prairie, broken by small irregular-shaped hills, which Lewis called 'The Prairie of the Knobs'. For the first time this year they were among abundant game; they were able not only to eat well but to start collecting and treating the skins they would probably need for bull-boats later on. The only blight was that they were plagued by mosquitoes which hummed round them and repeatedly bit them and their horses. They had to make huge smoky fires to keep the insects away so that they could get some rest.

Their Indian friends bade farewell to them, exchanging names as a token of friendship: Lewis became White Bearskin Folded, but he did not trouble to record which of his names he gave to the Indians. These peaceable Nez Percé told Lewis that he must now be very watchful because he was entering Blackfoot country. The Blackfeet, and their allies the Minnetarees of Fort de Prairie, were warlike and extremely treacherous. Now that the party was so much reduced in size, it would be very tempting to a Blackfoot war party. Still, there seemed no immediate danger. On 11 July, Lewis and his party arrived at White Bear Island above the Great Falls. The plains around them were thick with buffalo; Lewis estimated that there must have been something like ten thousand within a two-mile radius of the camp. He noted in his diary: 'it is now the season at which the buffaloe begin to coppelate and the bulls keep up a tremendous roaring'. The hunters had no difficulty in filling the larder; they shot eleven buffalo in one afternoon. It was essential that they should leave the boat party well supplied with meat, as all the skilled hunters were going with Lewis on his exploring trip.

Greatly to their disappointment, when they opened the cache by the Falls they discovered that they had underestimated the point to which the river waters would rise during the winter. The walls of the cache had half collapsed and the whole stock was thoroughly soaked. The bearskins they had left there had rotted away completely, and the specimens of plants and seeds were useless. One box of medicines was totally spoilt, as the stopper had come out of a bottle of laudanum and the contents had impregnated the other supplies. Luckily the map of the Missouri that Clark had prepared with such care was in good condition. They could not leave the remaining goods in this wet hole until the canoes arrived, so they built a scaffold hidden among some thick bushes on an island in the river and put everything on this. They were pleased, though, to find their old wheels which would ease the task of the main boat party when they carried their canoes past the Falls. Even with the wheels, though, it was going to be a back-breaking job to carry everything across. Lewis therefore changed his mind and cut his exploring party to four, himself and, inevitably, Drewyer and the Fields brothers, leaving Gass and the other two with horses to help in the portage. Gass would then take the horses by land to the mouth of Maria's river.

In all the circumstances cutting his numbers was a sensible thing to do, though it very nearly cost Lewis his life. What probably convinced him that he needed to leave a strong party behind was that McNeill had had a very narrow escape from a rampaging bear. He had been scouting through thick brush when his horse, frightened by the presence of a grizzly only ten feet away, threw him and galloped off. The bear instantly rose on to its hind legs and attacked. With great presence of mind McNeill, using his rifle as a club, hit the beast between the eyes, knocking it over and momentarily stunning it. While the bear rubbed his head perplexedly with its forepaws, McNeill, his rifle broken in half at the breach, ran to the nearest tree and clambered up it. The bear followed and circled round the tree expectantly until the light began to fade, when it lumbered off. After a watchful moment or two McNeill climbed down and ran back the two miles to camp to find his companions very worried because his horse had returned without him. It was so long since they had had a set-to with a grizzly that they had almost forgotten the dangers.

On 18 July, Lewis and his three companions set off to the point where Maria's river joined the Missouri and turned up the smaller river. For five days they explored the various branches of this river, until it became clear that there was no northern valley that would lead them up into Canada. All the water for Maria's river came down from the Rockies, not from the Canadian north. Disappointed, and thoroughly wet, since it was raining most of the time, Lewis headed back towards the Missouri. He was a little worried, for one day they

McNeill 'treed' by a prowling grizzly bear. His horse returning riderless to camp warned his companions that he was in trouble.

An American having struck a B

had seen a trail of fresh buffalo blood. They had not seen any Indians, but it was fairly obvious that there was a hunting-party somewhere in the neighbourhood, and probably Blackfeet at that. Lewis wrote in his diary: 'they are a vicious lawless and reather an abandoned set of wretches I wish to avoid an interview with them if possible.'

Unfortunately it was not possible. On the morning of 26 July, Lewis sent off Drewyer to hunt and climbed up on to a

it not kill'd him escapes into a Tree

high plain with the two Fields. Almost at once, about a mile ahead of them, they saw a small group of Indians – there turned out to be eight of them – and a much larger number of horses. The Indians were, as Lewis could see through his telescope, watching someone in the valley below them. This must almost certainly be Drewyer, so Lewis attracted their attention, going towards them with one of the Fields carrying the Stars and Stripes unfurled. One of the Indians rode up to examine them but without a word wheeled his horse and went back to the others. After a consultation all the Indians rode up to within a hundred yards of the explorers. Once again one came forward alone. Lewis went forward, also alone, and offered to shake hands. The Indian took his hand, and then as the rest of both parties came closer there was a general hand-shaking. By signs Lewis told them his intentions were friendly and he asked them who they were. He misunderstood the answer and believed that they were Minnetarees. In fact they were the even more ferocious Blackfeet. By much cautious sign conversation, which became more fluent as Drewyer, the expert, joined the party, they discovered that these eight men were a detachment of a much larger hunting-party, but this was some distance away. This made Lewis feel more confident. He thought he could cope with eight men, apparently armed only with two guns and a couple of war hatchets.

To keep an eye on them he suggested that they should all camp together; the Indians agreed to this, and together they cooked some of the buffalo meat that Drewyer had brought in with him. Until late that night they sat and smoked together. Lewis made hurried arrangements for one of his party to stay awake the whole time, and he himself took the first watch by the fire. The rest of the party retired with the Indians into their lodge and went to sleep. After a while, Lewis crept into the tent and woke Reuben Fields to take over the sentry duty. Lewis himself lay down and went to sleep. It is often said that this was a grave error of judgement on Lewis's part; he should not have slept that night at all, so that he could stay in control of the situation. I find it very hard to blame him for dropping off. After all, they were all nearly at the end of their resources, and if Fields had done his job properly the danger would not have been nearly so great.

However, they were outsmarted by the Indians. Just as it was getting light several of the Indians dashed out of the tent to where Reuben Fields was sitting rather drowsily by the fire. He had laid his and his brother's rifles on the ground beside him, and the Indians grabbed them. At the same time the other Indians seized Drewyer's and Lewis's guns which were beside them in the tent. With the true hunter's ability to wake up instantly, Drewyer immediately sprang up and wrestled with one of the Indians. After a chase and a further struggle he managed to get his gun back, but Lewis's was carried off.

A warrior of the fierce Blackfoot nation.
One of Bodmer's finest portraits.

187

Outside, Reuben Fields rather belatedly raised the alarm and chased after the man who was carrying his and his brother's guns. Showing a tremendous turn of speed, he caught up with the Indian and stabbed him with his hunting knife. The Indian staggered a few yards and then fell dead.

Three of the other Indians had rounded up the explorers' horses and were making off with them, calling on the others to join them. Lewis, now fully awake, chased after them with his pistol drawn while the Fields brothers started grabbing some of the loose horses to make sure that they had some means of escape. Lewis pointed his pistol at the Blackfoot who held his gun and signalled to him to drop it, which the Indian did. Drewyer, who came up beside Lewis at this point, wanted to shoot the man, but Lewis forbade him. Hearing the shouting, the Fields brothers now came up, but Lewis sent them back to secure as many horses as they could, sending Drewyer also to help them. The Indians were now circling round with the obvious intention of driving off all the horses. He gave Drewyer and the Fields brothers orders to shoot if necessary. He himself went unaccompanied in pursuit of the man who had stolen his gun, who, with a companion, was making off with a dozen horses away from the main group. They had not had time to mount, and Lewis pressed after them so hard that they let the horses go and turned to face him. One of them raised his gun. Lewis did not hesitate; he fired immediately, hitting the armed man in the stomach. The Indian fell, but at the same time he brought his gun up and fired back. Lewis heard the ball whistle past his head. He had no time to reload before the surviving Indian made off, leaving the horses. Lewis went back to the camp to look for the others. First Drewyer turned up, having rushed to the rescue when he heard the sound of the shots, and a little later the other two arrived, driving horses in front of them. They had chased the Indians for a while but these had broken up into two parties, one group swimming their horses across a river while the other rode off into the hills.

The immediate danger was over, and when the party rounded up the loose horses they found they were in fact better off than when the fighting started. They had lost one of their horses but had gained four Indian mounts. In addition they picked up a gun, four shields and two bows with their quivers of arrows as spoils of war. But it was certainly not safe to linger. The Blackfeet would undoubtedly try to link up with their

Captain Lewis shooting an Indian.

main force to the north and bring a full-scale war party to revenge their two dead comrades. The four men paused only to take a little buffalo meat and to recover the flag that they had given the Indians as a present the night before. Then they mounted Indian horses, which were in better condition than their own – fortunately all the saddles were still left – and galloped off.

Luckily the country was not too rough, so they were able to press forward at a full gallop. Indeed they did not stop until they had covered an estimated sixty-three miles, swimming a river forty yards wide on the way. The horses were then nearly exhausted, so they stopped for an hour and a half to rest them. They then rode another seventeen miles before making another halt as night fell. They stopped for a couple of hours, not only to rest the horses but to kill a buffalo which happened to be nearby, for food. There was enough moonlight for them to see their way, so they saddled up again and rode until two o'clock

ABOVE After Blackfoot Indians tried to make off with Lewis's gun and the party's horses, Lewis shot an escaping Indian, one of the few incidents of bloodshed during the expedition.

OVERLEAF 'Catching wild Horses' by George Catlin.

in the morning. Then being unable to go any farther, they lay
down to sleep. At first light they were all awake again, but they
were so stiff from their hours in the saddle that they could
scarcely ride their horses. Before struggling to mount, they held
a short council of war. The Blackfeet, Lewis guessed, would
head for the point where Maria's river joined the Missouri.
His party had two alternatives. They could head across country
to a point below where the rivers joined, which would take all

'Escape from the Blackfeet' by Alfred Jacob Miller. Lewis and his companions rode for sixty-three miles without drawing rein to escape Indian pursuit.

day and might well put the canoe party in danger, since it might be ambushed by the Indians at Maria's river; or they could head straight for the Missouri and try to meet the canoe party before it reached the danger point. Lewis told his companions that they must be prepared to risk their lives for the sake of the larger party by heading direct for the Missouri. If there were no sign of the canoes, they would leave their baggage, cross the river by raft and work their way upstream until they met the canoes.

Wearily they climbed on to their horses again. On Lewis's instructions they tied their bridles together, so that if they were attacked as they rode across the open plains to the big river it would not be possible for the Indians to separate them and pick them off one by one. They would escape or die together. Off they galloped, and after twelve miles they knew they were not far from the river. In the distance they heard a sound that might have been a shot. Could this be the boat party, or were the Indians by some terrible chance ahead of them? It was a risk that they had to take, so they rode straight towards the point from which the shot seemed to have come. They carried on for another eight miles and then heard the familiar sounds of the hunting guns. As they rode up to the river, they were greeted by the cheerful sight of the canoes coming round a bend to meet them. Hastily Lewis turned their horses loose, and they loaded their baggage on to the canoes and pushed off. Within an hour or two, Gass and the two men who were bringing the reserve horses down the river turned up. The whole party made its way without seeing another Indian to the place where they had made their first cache and hidden the red pirogue.

Here again the cache had fallen in and much of the supplies they had left behind were spoiled. Some of the food was in good condition and they took on board all that was worth saving. The red pirogue, however, was completely rotted, so they continued to use the five canoes to supplement the white pirogue, which had been found intact. There was room enough for them all, though the journey would have been more comfortable in the bigger boat. They did not mind this much, as they had come through the most difficult part of the journey and were going downstream towards home. In fact they made very good speed and covered the four hundred miles to the mouth of the Yellowstone in eleven days, their best day's passage being eighty-three miles.

9 The Last Leg

WHEN THEY ARRIVED at the mouth of the Yellowstone on 7 August Clark was not there to meet them, but they found tied to a pole a piece of paper bearing Lewis's name in Clark's handwriting; the rest had disintegrated. Nearby was a camp-site which had obviously been abandoned a few days before, and here they found a fragment of another note saying that Clark had gone ahead and would meet them lower down. What had happened was that the ever-efficient Clark had accomplished his trip so easily, and without the hair-raising adventures of his fellow-commander, that he had arrived early at the rendezvous, but since he could find little game thereabouts he had set off to look for better hunting-grounds.

In the month that had elapsed since he had left Lewis at Traveller's Rest, he had been on the move the whole time. He had worked his way up to the Shoshone villages and there had found that the cache was in excellent condition and the canoes serviceable when dried out. The tobacco chewers among the party, who had had no supplies since Christmas – the formal smokings since then had been in 'Indian' tobacco, various mixtures of local leaves and herbs – were so keen to help themselves from the cached supplies that they did not bother to unsaddle their horses before digging for tobacco.

After a short rest at the village, they led their horses along the Jefferson river while the supplies went down by canoe, until the time came – at Three Forks – for the canoe party that was to pick up Lewis to go towards the Great Falls, while Clark with his detachment of ten men with Sacajawea and her papoose rode off through the mountains to find the nearest point of the Yellowstone. It was Sacajawea who acted as guide, for she had been over the gap in the mountains as a child. This gap was later called the Bozeman Pass; it was the route used by many of those who made their way into the north-west some fifty years later.

Somewhat to their surprise, they found that the Yellowstone was navigable from the point where they arrived at its banks. Clark set about there and then making a craft that was a combination of canoe and raft. He told the men to hollow out a pair of thirty-two-foot-long tree trunks and lash them together with a sort of platform in the middle to carry the luggage. This was a very useful vessel for going downstream, and they made very good speed on it. It was fortunate that they were able to contrive boat space for most of the party, for they were

OPPOSITE Upper Falls of the Yellowstone river, as painted by James Moran.

196

Crow Indians proved adept at stealing horses from the expedition and were to become the most skilful horse thieves in the West.

conscious that there were Indians about. Charbonneau thought that he saw one standing on a cliff in the distance, and there were smoke signals. They saw no one, but during the night of 20 July twenty-four of their horses disappeared. (They had been stolen by Crow Indians, who in later years would prove to be the most accomplished horse thieves in the West, as many later settlers were to find to their cost.)

Clark decided to stick to the river, but he sent Pryor with three men to drive their remaining stock of horses overland to the Mandan villages. He was to sell them there to provide money for the rest of the journey, and in addition was to contact Mr Heney of the North West Company and ask him to bring the Sioux in for a further meeting, and if possible persuade one of their chiefs to go to Washington. As it happened, all Pryor's stock of horses was stolen within two days by the Crows. Still, with the admirable ingenuity displayed by every member of the expedition, he got himself and his companions out of trouble. They killed a buffalo and from its skin built two bull-boats – the coracle-like craft they had seen among the Mandans – and floated down the river in them, arriving at its mouth only four days after Clark.

Soon after parting from Pryor, Clark saw a huge rock covered with Indian paintings close to the river. He went ashore to examine it and carved his name on its surface – a signature that can be seen today. He called the rock Pompey's Pillar in honour of Sacajawea's son who had acquired the name Pompey in the last week or so. The rest of the journey passed without incident, though it was uncomfortable because of the incessant rain. When they reached the point where the rivers joined they made camp to await Lewis, but this was no place to stay – the mosquitoes were terrible and food was short. They moved slowly on down the river. A week later they saw a canoe with two white men in it – but coming from the wrong direction. These were, in fact, the trappers Dixon and Hancock, who were coming up the Missouri. They were the first white men anyone from the expedition had seen since 13 April of the year before. There was, they reported, trouble farther down the river: the peace that Lewis and Clark had proposed when with the Mandans had not lasted long. The Minnetarees and the Mandans were attacking the Aricaras, and the Sioux were making a nuisance of themselves with all and sundry.

Pompey's pillar, the huge rock named after Sacajawea's son where Clark's initials can still be seen carved on the rock face.

Clark thought that it would be better to wait for Lewis at this point. He did not have to wait long. The next day five canoes came into sight; the crews yelled out on seeing him, though the sound did not appear quite as cheerful as it should have done. In fact, the one really serious accident of the trip had occurred the day before. It is true that other people had been hurt; they had fallen and gashed themselves, put out their shoulders hauling heavy loads and suffered from many minor ailments, but there had been nothing like this. On 11 August, the day before they had arrived at Clark's present camp, Lewis had gone ashore to hunt elk. Only Cruzatte, the boatman, was with him. Lewis tells what happened in his diary:

We fired on the elk I killed one and he wounded another, we reloaded our guns and took different routs through the thick willows in pursuit of the Elk; I was in the act of firing on the Elk a second time when a ball struck my left thye about an inch below my hip joint, missing the bone it passed through the left thye and out the thickness of the bullet across the hinder part of my right thye; the stroke was very severe; I instantly supposed that Cruzatte had shot me in mistake for an Elk as I was dressed in brown leather and he cannot see very well; under this impression I called out to him damn you, you have shot me.

Though he went on shouting, there was no reply, and no sign of Cruzatte. Suddenly Lewis was convinced that he must have been attacked by Indians. Picking up his gun, he staggered through the undergrowth back to the boat to get help to rescue Cruzatte who, he was convinced, must have been captured. As an armed party swarmed ashore Lewis tried to go with them, but his wound was too painful. They must, he shouted after them, try to rescue the boatman, but if the Indians were present in too great numbers they were to conduct a fighting retreat to the shore. In twenty minutes they were back: it had all been a ghastly accident. There were no Indians, only Cruzatte. He had fired only once after he and Lewis separated, and was convinced he had aimed at an elk. He had not heard Lewis calling him, and could not believe that he had wounded his commander. Nothing would convince him until he was shown the bullet, which had been caught in Lewis's breeches and clearly came from his gun.

Sadly they carried Lewis on board and, having tended his wound as best they could, set off with all speed to catch up

Clark. The next day they found him. Lewis then made the last entry in his diary:

My wounds felt very stiff and soar this morning but gave me no considerable pain. there was much less inflamation than I had any reason to apprehend there would be . . . at 1 p.m. I overtook Capt Clark and party and had the pleasure of finding them all well, as wrighting in my present situation is very painfull to me I shall desist untill I recover and leave to my frined Capt C. the continuation of our journal.

There was not a great deal more to say. In four days they were at the Mandan villages, where they received a great welcome. On the face of it everything seemed very peaceful. One Eye, Big White and the other chiefs were all there to meet them. Clark did all the talking, since Lewis was still in great pain; he passed out the first day they were there when Clark changed the dressing on the wound, but he began to improve and within a week or ten days was able to hobble a little.

Clark's task was to persuade the chiefs of the various tribes to go with them to Washington to make their submission to the President in person. Big White consented to go if his wives and family could come with him, so they prepared a vessel for him from two canoes lashed together, and Jessaume, the Frenchman who lived with the Mandans, agreed to go along to interpret. The Minnetarees absolutely refused to send any-one. This was a sad blow to the expedition, as Charbonneau had intended to go with them to St Louis as interpreter for the Minnetarees, but when the Indians refused there was no point in his making the journey. Clark tried to persuade him, but he said there would be no work for him downriver; he would be happier staying behind. Clark offered to take little Pompey, now a 'beautifull boy' of nineteen months. Sacajawea refused this offer, but said perhaps he might come down when he was a year older in order to be educated in a white man's world. So sadly Charbonneau was paid off, and handsomely, with the strange sum of five hundred dollars, thirty-three and one-third cents.

Coulter also took his discharge at this point. He had met some trappers and was keen to try his luck up the Yellowstone again. The rest packed up and made ready to set off. As a parting present, Clark gave one of the big swivel guns to One Eye. He had it set up in the centre of the village, saying

Village of the Minnatarees.

with great solemnity that this represented the voice of the Great White Father and that when it spoke men would listen. They showed One Eye how to load it and he ceremoniously fired it.

On 17 August, a final council was held with much pipe-smoking and many farewell speeches. The whole party embarked and, to the sound of howling women, set off down the river. They made good speed with the current helping them, but, though they were keen to get back to St Louis, they stopped several times to hold councils with tribes by the river. Some, such as the Cheyenne, they had not met on the way up. They handed one of their few remaining medals to Grey Eyes, the chief of this people. He seems to have been the only chief they met who did not want a medal; he handed it back hurriedly with a present for Clark of a buffalo-skin robe and some meat, saying he feared that the medal was 'bad medicine'. Clark, however, reassured him, telling him it was the symbol of the White Father's sincerity, after which Grey Eyes wore it happily.

A few days later, near where they had had the brush with the Teton Sioux two winters before, they saw some Tetons on the bank. Through an interpreter Clark shouted a message that the Great White Father would not forget their conduct, and that if they did not behave themselves they would be punished. When the Indians begged for corn they were sent away empty-handed. A short while later the travellers heard gunfire and saw a large band of Indians lining the shore. The boat party immediately made ready for battle. Lewis even hobbled ashore to direct operations. But it was a false alarm; these were Yanktons, not Tetons, and quite friendly. They had been practising shooting at a keg in the river, hence the gunfire.

After that it was an easy run all the way. The Missouri was much more crowded than when they started up it in 1804. They met quite a few traders, who gave them the news that there was now a large force of American troops stationed at St Louis and that other explorers were setting out. Soon after they had been ashore to pay their respects at Sergeant Floyd's tomb – it had been desecrated by Indians, but they filled in the disturbed grave and left it tidy – they met an old friend of Clark's, Robert McClelan, who was travelling upriver to explore where the impulse took him. One of the tasks that had been set him was to discover what trace he could find of the Lewis and Clark expedition, which had been totally given up for lost by the authorities in Washington, no word having been

Mandan Chief in full regalia.

heard from it for eighteen months. McClelan had some whisky with him, so the expedition had its first tot for more than a year. It then sped on its way to inform the world that its members were still alive.

On 23 September, St Louis finally came into sight and the weary men rowed their way across the Mississippi into the harbour. It was seven hundred and seventy days since they started.

10
'Deserved Well
of their Country'

THE FIRST LETTER that Lewis wrote when he landed was to his old patron, Thomas Jefferson, at the White House. On 2 December 1806, the President sent the following message to Congress:

The expedition of Messrs Lewis and Clark, for exploring the river Missouri, and the best communication from that to the Pacific Ocean, has had all the success which could have been expected. They have traced the Missouri nearly to its source, descended the Columbia to the Pacific Ocean, ascertained with accuracy the geography of that interesting communication across our continent, learned the character of the country, of its commerce, and inhabitants; and it is but justice to say that Messrs Lewis and Clark, and their brave companions, have by this arduous service deserved well of their country.

They had indeed, and this time Congress did not quibble. The men who had refused to grant Clark a captain's commission when he set out were now happy to make him a general in the militia and Agent General for Indian Affairs for Louisiana. He married his Julia, who bore him five children before she died in 1820, perhaps from exhaustion. He married again a year later and had two more children. In the meantime he was given many other official posts around St Louis, most of them connected with Indian affairs, and he was also Governor of the Illinois Territory. So great was his influence among the Indians that they always referred to St Louis as 'The Red-Head's Town'. His slave York was granted his freedom on the expedition's arrival back and became a well-known figure in St Louis, famous for his tall stories of his adventures with the Indians.

Of the subsequent history of most of the members of the expedition not so much is known. Pryor is thought to have become an ensign in the American army. Certainly someone of the same name and with that rank took a party of visiting Indian chiefs back up the Missouri. Gass, the carpenter and opportunist, took his diary to a local schoolmaster and with his help was the first to achieve print with his story, full of inaccuracies, in 1809. Later he took to drink for a while, but then saw the light and became a preacher back in his native West Virginia. Drewyer, the half-breed, returned up the Missouri and is buried somewhere in Montana.

Charbonneau stayed around with the Mandans for another thirty years and was still there when Prince Maximilian of Wied and his party came up by steamboat. Still by the side of this boastful old man was the quiet figure of his Shoshone wife.

PREVIOUS PAGE Meriwether Lewis and William Clark.

208

The Prince thought her a rather pathetic sight, dressed in European clothes and 'aping the ways of European women'. Soon after this meeting Charbonneau died, and within a few years Sacajawea had reverted to Indian life again. She married a Comanche and disappeared from the European settlements, but it is known that she lived to be over ninety. She must often have felt bitter, having lived on to see those who followed in the footsteps of the explorers she had served so well, and who in their off-hand way were so fond of her, massacre her people and drive them from their lands. Perhaps it is a national guilty conscience that has raised her to the status of a folk-heroine on a level with Pocohontas and often ascribes to her a far bigger role in the expedition than the diaries of the leaders justify. She was, as far as is known, the last survivor of the expedition, dying on 9 April 1884.

Alexis Charbonneau who claimed to be descended from Sacajawea's son Pompey.

There is no record of what happened to 'Little Pompey', that much-travelled papoose. He was not sent down the river to be educated under Clark's patronage. The only possible clue to his life is a record that one 'Jack Charbonneau', a half-breed, died along with the rest of his party while on a prospecting trip in the Colorado desert. This may have been Pompey.

And what of Meriwether Lewis, the man who stood to gain most from the success of the expedition? First a triumphant return; all Washington at his feet; a President delighted to be presented with results beyond almost anything he could have hoped for. Even Congress was grateful. For a while everything seemed to go well. Lewis was immediately appointed Governor of the whole of the Louisiana Territory. After staying in Washington for some time, writing his reports in full and starting the task of turning his diary notes into a narrative of the expedition, he returned to St Louis. This time he was not the returning hero but the representative of government sent to bring order to an area that had no great liking for authority. The feuding traders, some of them French and some of them new arrivals from the United States, were not as easy to deal with as the Indians of the Far West, but in two years (February 1807 to October 1809) Lewis succeeded in bringing a certain amount of order to the region and set in train important territorial reforms.

It looked as if the young governor had a great career before him. With his reputation as the man who had opened up the West, there is no reason why he should not have eventually followed his patron into the White House. But something snapped: by the summer of 1809 he was suffering from constant attacks of real or imagined sickness, and his mind was beginning to wander. His enemies in St Louis seized upon some minor irregularities in the official accounts and sent reports on them to Washington. Anxiety about this made Lewis's condition far worse, and he was in a precarious mental state when he set off for Washington to discuss the financial problem. He journeyed to the place where Memphis, Tennessee, now stands. From here he was to have continued his trip by boat, but he suddenly changed his mind and rode off accompanied by Neely, the local Indian agent, and a couple of servants. After a day's travelling, two of the horses were lost. While Neely rounded them up Lewis rode on ahead to the nearest house, a farm belonging to a man called Grinder. Like most places on the trails through Indian country, the farm was always prepared to put up visitors. Lewis hired a room, while his servants were housed in an outbuilding.

No one knows quite what happened next. The official version, the one that President Jefferson recorded in his memoir of Lewis, states that Lewis's mind finally snapped and that some time in the early hours of the morning he shot himself. Mrs Grinder gave several different accounts, including one macabre version according to which Lewis only wounded himself originally and lingered on through the night, raving, before he finished himself off. All that is known is that he was shot with his own gun. It is, however, widely believed that he was murdered, probably by the Grinders. He was carrying with him a large number of boxes, which contained not only documents relative to his financial troubles but the diaries of the expedition. In his disturbed mental state Lewis had shown an obsessive concern for the safety of these boxes, so Neely, who is generally regarded as a reliable witness, tells us. It might well be that the Grinders thought that the boxes contained valuables and killed Lewis to get hold of them, cooking up the suicide story afterwards when the contents proved worthless.

It does not really matter which story is true: Lewis's end was in any case tragic. He lived only three years and eighteen days after the expedition returned in triumph to St Louis. He was buried where he died on the lonely farm in Tennessee, and forty years later the local people raised a monument to him there. But his true monument is the official history of

OPPOSITE The deed under which Congress granted Meriwether Lewis 1600 acres of land west of the Mississippi.

No. 𝟏

Pursuant to an act of congress passed on the 3d day of March, 1807, entitled "An act making compensation to Messieurs Lewis and Clarke and their companions," *Meriwether Lewis* _____ is entitled to

One thousand, six hundred Acres of Land

to be located agreeably to said act, at the option of the holder or possessor, " with any register or registers of the land offices, subsequent to the public sales in such office, on any of the public lands of the United States, lying on the west side of the Mississippi, then and there offered for sale, or may be received at the rate of two dollars per acre, in payment of any such lands."

Given at the War-office this *sixth* day of *March* in the year one thousand eight hundred and seven.

Registered:

H. Dearborn

Secretary of war.

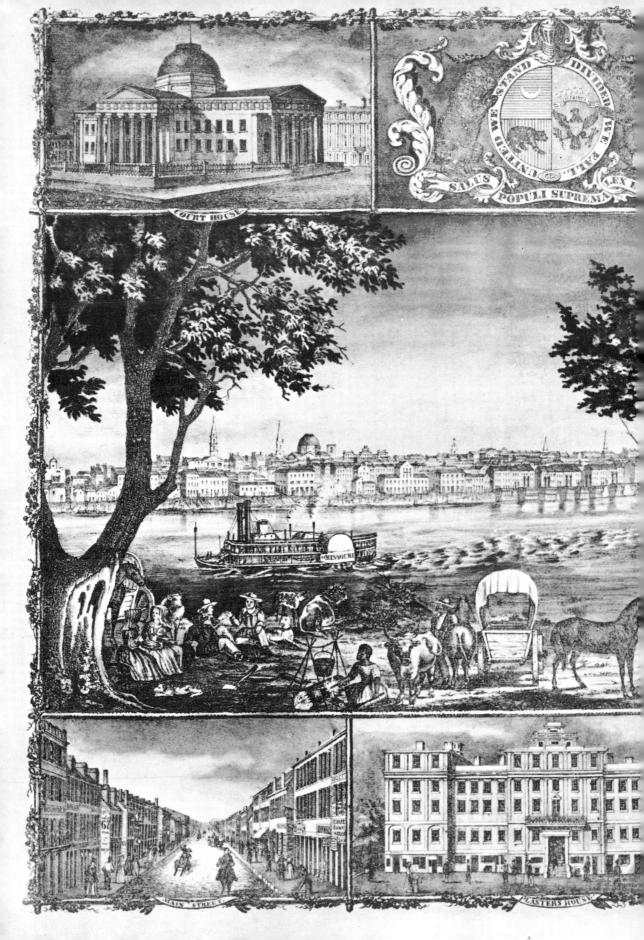

COURT HOUSE.

UNITED WE STAND DIVIDED WE FALL

SALUS POPULI SUPREMA LEX ESTO

MISSOURI

MAIN STREET.

PLANTERS HOUSE.

When the expedition returned they found that the village of St Louis was already growing into a town and soon it was one of the main trading ports of the Mississippi and Missouri water routes. It was also a regular collecting point for those who were making the journey by land.

This lithograph shows St Louis in the mid 1800s, with the principal buildings of that time featured round the border; picture by courtesy of Chicago Historical Society.

the expedition based on the diaries kept by Lewis and Clark.

This was not published until six years after Lewis's death. It had been his intention to write the book himself, but he had done no more than the preliminary sorting. It was obvious that Clark could not undertake the task. As the extracts from his diaries show, he could write vividly, but he was barely literate; and in any case he had better things to do with his time. The task was given to Nicholas Biddle, a Philadelphia lawyer, who was given the diaries and also the assistance of young Shannon, the man who was always getting lost. In addition constant appeals were made to Clark to clarify points of detail.

In the end, so much time elapsed between the return of the expedition and the publication of the book that public interest had waned, so that the first publication was a financial loss. Now, though it has few literary graces, it remains one of the great documents of travel literature. President Theodore Roosevelt, a man who knew his American north-west well and wrote one of the classic histories of it, *The Winning of the West*, wrote: 'Few explorers who did and saw so much that was actually new have written of their deeds with such quiet absence of boastfulness, and have drawn their descriptions with such freedom of exaggeration.'

This, I think, exactly sums things up: the expedition had no pretensions. A bunch of tough men set out to make their way across America, by water when they could, to note down all that they saw on the way, to make a map and then to report to the President. They carried out their task to the letter and with an efficiency that is unparalleled in the history of exploration. By the standards of many explorations, the party was large, yet on the way only one man was lost, and he died from a condition that was incurable at that time and from which he was presumably suffering before the party set out. It was even more remarkable that while travelling through often hostile country they managed to avoid bloodshed until that one fatal morning when a moment's lack of vigilance led to the killing of two Indians. Their hardships were immense, yet their spirits remained unaffected. It was a text-book journey in that Lewis and Clark almost without exception controlled events and did not allow their plans to be upset. Yet their approach was not so rigid that they took absurd risks just to keep to their schedule.

And what did they prove? First, a negative: there was no North-West Passage by river that would bring the riches of the

As the century advanced, immigrants made
their way into the western territories.
Most hoped to get rich quickly, others
wanted only to make a better life than
they had. The stubborn stayed to build
a new life and future.

News of the discovery of silver attracted a rush of prospectors.
Placer miners, as shown here, worked with pick, shovel and shallow pans
along the gravel beds of streams; illustration by O. C. Seltzer.

The redoubtable mountain men, like the one illustrated
here by O.C. Seltzer, usually worked alone, often facing hunger and
Indian attack as they searched for beaver.

Zebulon Pike (1779–1813) explored the South-western trails while Lewis and Clark were heading north-west. Pike's Peak is named after him. He was killed in the War of 1812.

West to the Atlantic seaboard. This was a dream, but they did bring the first word of a whole new landscape, great plains thick with buffalo, high mountains and streams crowded with beaver. They showed that there were ways through the Rocky Mountains. The route they took, of course, was not the only one. Indeed when the great westward migration started forty years later, the people who headed first for the great plains and then on to California took a route far to the south of the one Lewis and Clark pioneered. Even while their trip was on, Zebulon Pike was prospecting along the Arkansas river and circling round down through the Spanish south-west. But the beaver traders and the mountain men who held sway in the north-west followed in the footsteps of Lewis and Clark, and so later did railway builders. One thing escaped Lewis and Clark, as they struggled with their canoes through the canyons of what is now Montana. They did not notice that the creeks which poured into the river from the north were bearing down with them a quantity of alluvial silver. Sixty years later, those same canyons were crawling with prospectors.

The great achievement of Lewis and Clark is that they brought back word to a people who had clung to the Atlantic seaboard for two centuries that the whole continent was theirs and offered rewards beyond belief for anyone brave enough to earn them. Lewis and Clark have as much a claim as Columbus to be discoverers of America.

Select Bibliography

Original Journals of the Lewis and Clark Expedition, edited by Reuben Gold Thwaites. 8 vols (New York, 1904)

History of the Expedition under the Command of Lewis and Clark, edited by Elliott Coues. 3 vols (New York, 1965)

The Journals of Lewis and Clark, edited by Bernard de Voto (Boston, 1953)

The Trail of Lewis and Clark, Olin D. Wheeler (New York, 1904)

American Odyssey: the Journey of Lewis and Clark, Ingvard Henry Eide (Chicago, 1969)

Westward the Course of Empire, Bernard de Voto (London, 1954)

The American West, John A. Hawgood (London, 1967)

The American Heritage Book of Indians, edited by Alvin M. Josephy Jr (London, 1968)

The Art of the American West, Paul A. Rossi and David C. Hunt (London, 1972)

The American West, Larry J. Curry (London, 1972)

The Penguin Book of the American West, David Lavender (London, 1969)

The Winning of the West, Theodore Roosevelt (New York, 1964)

Letters and Notes on the Manners, Customs and Conditions of North American Indians, George Catlin (New York, 1973)

Acknowledgements

Photographs and illustrations were supplied by or are reproduced by kind permission of the following:

British Museum 40*a* & *b*, 41*a* & *b*, 49, 78, 100, 136, 137, 143;

Chicago Historical Society 212–13;

Denver Public Library, Western History Department 23, 34–5, 36, 37, 43, 46–7, 61, 62–3, 68, 70–1, 74, 75, 76, 77, 86–7, 96, 102–3. 109, 115, 125, 133, *145b*, *148a*, 152*a*, 157*a*, *160*, 168–9, 173, 174–5, 181, 187, 194–5, 198, 199, 202–3, 205, 209, 216;

Fort Clatsop National Memorial, Oregon 158;

The Thomas Gilcrease Institute of American History and Art *2*, *3*, *14–15*, *82a* & *b*, *83a* & *b*, *94–5*, 98, 101, 116–17, 128–9, *145a*, *148b*, 150, *157b*, 176, *178–9*, *190–1*, 197, 215, 216, 217;

Historical Pictures Service, Chicago 10–11, 13, 19, 21, 52–3, 65, 66, 80, 104, 107, 120;

Missouri Historical Society 84, 89;

Montana Historical Society 56–7, 112–13, 119, 134–5;

The National Archives and Records Service, Washington 12, 165, 211;

The National Gallery of Canada, Ottawa 18;

Oregon State Highway Division 146–7;

Radio Times Hulton Picture Library 26–7, 31, 54, 90, 140–1, 152*b*, 171–2, 184–5, 189;

The St Louis Art Museum 25;

The Science Museum, London (Crown copyright 162*a*), 162*b*, 163*a*;

The Smithsonian Institution 163*b*;

The Walters Art Gallery 50, 122–3, 192.

Index

Captain Clark and his me